This Time in the Church

Text copyright © 2015 remains with the authors and for the collection with ATF Theology. All rights reserved. Except for any fair dealing permitted under the Copyright Act, no part of the publication may be reproduced by any means without prior permission. Inquiries should be made in the first instance with the publisher.

A Forum for Theology in the World
Volume 2, Issue 1, 2015

A Forum for Theology in the World is an academic refereed journal aimed at engaging with issues in the contemporary world, a world which is pluralist and eucumenical in nature. The journal reflects this pluralism and ecumenism. Each edition is theme specific and has its own editor responsible for the production. The journal aims to elicit and encourage dialogue on topics and issues in contemporary society and within a variety of religious traditions. The Editor in Chief welcomes submissions of manuscripts, collections of articles, for review from individuals or institutions, which may be from seminars or conferences or written specifically for the journal. An internal peer review is expected before submitting the manuscript. It is the expectation of the publisher that, once a manuscript has been accepted for publication, it will be submitted according to the house style to be found at the back of this volume. All submissions to the Editor in Chief are to be sent to: hdregan@atf.org.au.

Each edition is available as a journal subscription, or as a book in print, pdf or epub, through the ATF Press web site — www.atfpress.com. Journal subscriptions are also available through EBSCO and other library suppliers.

Editor in Chief
Hilary Regan, ATF Press

A Forum for Theology in the World is published by ATF Theology and imprint of
ATF (Australia) Ltd (ABN 90 116 359 963) and
is published twice or three times a year.
ISSN 1329-6264

ATF Press
PO Box 504
Hindmarsh SA 5007
Australia
www.atfpress.com

Subscription Rates 2015

Print	On-Line	Print and On-line
Aust $65 Individuals	Aus $55 individuals	Aus $75 individuals
Aus $90 Institutions	Aus $80 individuals	Aus $100 instiutions

This Time in the Church

edited by Michael Kelly SJ

ATF Theology
Adelaide
2015

Forum for Theology in the World Vol 2 No 1/2015

Contents

	Introduction	vii
1	This Time in the Church *Michael Kelly SJ*	1
2	Our Church Further Down the Track *Christopher Geraghty*	15
3	Good News and Bad News in the Church *Fr Frank Brennan SJ*	73
	Contributors	99

Forum for Theology in the World Vol 2 No 1/2015

Introduction

I remember the 1980s well. It was a time in the Catholic Church when the first flush of enthusiasm for what Vatican II brought to the Church was just about spent. But overall, there looked to be bright prospects and a fairly clear road for reform.

The perennial tensions in a worldwide entity such as the Catholic Church were very evident, especially in the misunderstandings between the centre and periphery, with people in the field and the generals at headquarters (Rome) sharing a mutual incomprehension. There was the fallout from *Humanae Vitae* where some Catholics learnt for the first time that the assertion *Roma loquitur, causa finita est* (Rome has spoken, that's the end of the matter) isn't all it's cracked up to be.

But in Australia at least, it seemed all systems go. Mass attendance in parishes seemed to be holding and parishes were busy. The ministries of the Church, especially education and health care, were growing exponentially, fueled by new money from state and federal governments. Entries to seminaries and religious congregations, while down on the boom times up to the mid 1960s, were still flowing at a sustainable rate. The international Church was being led by an internationally respected figure in the first Slavic pope who seemed to have it in mind to liberate his people and even bring the Soviet empire to its knees.

From the 1990s on, it all seems to have gone in another direction and to the eyes of some, gone horribly wrong. It has been the experience of the central authority in Rome, amplified through its repeater stations in local bishops that frequently neither listened to nor seemed to care what ordinary Catholics think or experience or really believe; it has meant a ceremonial form of Catholic worship that left many Catholics wondering what sort of circus they had let themselves in to see; attitudes of judgment and dismissal from Church authorities that closed down conversations about meaning, mission and purpose because those who thought they could close down the conversations appeared not to want to hear anything but a chorus of approval for their views; the creation of an elite form of Catholicism as the only form of Catholicism if you wanted a say in how things were done.

Then came sex abuse. Sex, in all its moods and senses, had become the most publicised subject in Roman teaching, a measure of orthodoxy and the constant preoccupation of national hierarchies in their public profiles. For a global community so preoccupied with putting the world to rights on the subject, to have it revealed that its own house was abysmally disordered brought that form of 'leadership' into disrepute.

That's where the discussions at the 'Camino Series', held at St Mary's North Sydney, through 2013, found their starting point. The facts are now well known and need no repeating. The subject of the first paper by me is not the scandal itself but where does the Church as a community and a public entity, need to go from here.

That discussion—as intimate as it is related to some very public features of the Church—has a context: the history of a Church badly in need of structural reform. If the sentiments of the faithful and the desire to make the community of the Church more in deed what it claims in words, the reach of those changes is as profound as it is extensive. Effective reform of an historical community like the Roman Catholic Church will not happen without a deep grasp of the history of forms in need of reformation. That is the focus of Chris Geraghty's contribution.

Probing the spirit and reforming the body are for a purpose: mission. That mission is conditioned by the challenges of the context in which it is exercised. That is the focus of Frank Brennan's contribution as he assesses the challenges and proposes some fresh approaches to meeting them. Because there have been so many formulaic and essentially unengaged responses to contemporary issues in and beyond the Church, the transformation needed in attitude and practical proposals to handle them is vast.

But this series of talks was given through a year of extraordinary surprises that have happened since Pope Benedict resigned and Pope Francis became Bishop of Rome, as he likes to title himself. Even if it's only catching up with many things that have become commonplace assumptions in the contemporary world, it would seem that the Catholic Church is at a turning point.

Such a turn of events only serves to vindicate the view of an early twentieth century French Church poet and writer, Charles Peguy, who once remarked that at the turn of an age, the Church always arrives a little late and a little breathless.

For believers, the future belongs not to fears but to God. The only authentic and spiritually persuasive response to being in the middle of a change of eras like this is one that allows the Spirit to do what the Spirit does. And what the Spirit does is always surprise. Discipleship asks that we be attentive to the unexpected ways we may be drawn.

Being alert to God's initiative does not absolve us of the responsibility to be strategic in the way we respond to the Spirit.

One currently proposed response to this change of eras adopted by some in the Church, and reinforced by Emeritus Pope Benedict, is quite happy to welcome this age as one of decline in the Church as we have known it. It is seen as a God given opportunity to scale the Church back to a faithful remnant that would be distinctive because of its orthodoxy and compliance with what Rome and its utterances required as has happened under the management of the last three decades.

Shame about the mass of Catholics, you might say. They can amuse themselves. There is the elite and that's all there really needs to be any concern for.

The more recent, but also more ancient, view—proposed by Pope Francis who also accepts a reduced size and presence of the Church as inevitable and perhaps desirable—is to say that elitism is for the birds and what is needed is for the Church to be present and make its contribution as leaven: distinctive, even vital and decisive, but not all consuming and dominating.

The faithful remnant—and not the usual clerical and religious suspects—in this view will be distinctive because it engages directly with the issues and concerns that the average person has, is in the market place and is ready to give an account of the hope they have. It is not hidden away behind sacristy doors and locked into conversations with the already signed up membership.

However the present becomes the future, one thing is sure: what is ahead won't be like the past. We might just be in a situation right now, if the challenges detailed in this 'Camino Series' are any indication, of such abject poverty and resourcelessness that we might be more open to allow God to be God.

This Time in the Church

Michael Kelly SJ

I chose the title 'This Time in The Church' for my paper because it specifies exactly what I would like you to consider. It also happens to be the title of an excellent and very short book by one of the unsung heroes of the Australian Church, Melbourne priest Frank O'Loughlin.

The book is one about the shift in context for the Church in the Western world today and its impact on what the Church now plainly is—a pluralist, multifaceted and unalterably diverse community, and a long way from the perception common in the media and in many Catholics' imagination of a monolithic, monochrome, monolingual and absolutist entity, centrally administered with military effect everywhere as a chain of command acts locally on a compliant membership.

You should read the book. But I have chosen the title because it specifies two points I want to focus on—the Australian Church and its predicament right now. I agree with Philip Wilson, the present Archbishop of Adelaide who, prior to that appointment, did a sterling job to clean up an ecclesiastical catastrophe—the Diocese of Wollongong. He was twice elected President of the Australian Bishops Conference and would still hold that position if allowed a third term by its rules, such was his leadership of the bishops and his reading among them of the challenges the Australian Church faces.

Wilson has nominated the abuse crisis as the biggest crisis in the history of the Church in Australia. But such a claim is not new. Its outline was given many years ago in the first report on the Australian Church's response to the abuse crisis—*Towards Healing*.

In 1997, Bishop Geoffrey Robinson perceptively observed that the abuse crisis was only partly to do with the criminal acts of some who visited their evil on the innocent and unsuspecting. It was also something that was intimately connected to the unhealthy culture in the Church at many levels—not just the culture of secrecy and practices by hierarchs but the clericalism that fostered that culture, the training of clergy in isolated, all-male institutions and the destructive ideas that have been part of the Church's self-understanding for centuries, even millennia—attitudes to the body, to sex, to women and to authority in Church.

'Let the process of investigation and correction end where it will' was Bishop Geoffrey Robinson's view and he has filled it out in a couple of books, one of which earned the censure of Australia's bishops.

Of course, the Church has faced many challenges in the past. The Second Vatican Council was the long overdue way in which the Catholic Church addressed its irrelevance. Since the French Revolution, the European world had changed mightily. But until the 1960s, the Catholic Church's official response to many of those changes was that the world was in error. Systematically opposing the impact of liberalism, democracy, the fact of many conscientiously committed Christians in non-Catholic Churches, the enduring life and faith of the Jews, advances in science, in the understanding and interpretation of ancient documents such as the Scriptures and Church doctrines, the impact of industrialisation and the end of the European colonial era, one during which Roman Catholicism became the only section of the Christian Church to effectively globalise, the Catholic Church, despite its smug confidence in itself as the one true faith, had some issues to address. Principally, in the face of all these world-shaping changes, the relevance of Catholic Christianity was under strain.

But the present challenge to which Wilson and Robinson point is an even more profound one than questioning the cultural relevance of Catholic Christianity. This time in the Church is a challenge to and a questioning of its credibility—moral and spiritual—and not just in Australia but North America and Europe also.

Currently, to address immediate issues and create a public response, the Australian Church has two bodies that offer the formal framework for a response to the crisis of sexual abuse. The crisis is as much about the criminal behaviour of a number of psychopaths in the employ of the Church—clergy, religious and lay people working in Catholic institutions—as it is about the mismanagement of the incidents, the perpetrators of the deeds and the victims of these incidents by Church leaders—episcopal and in religious congregations.

But the crisis is not like the discovery of fraud and embezzlement in a Church institution. That is a crime with a beginning, a middle and an end. These are always localised crimes whose history can be traced, whose evidence is always tangible and whose resolution is effected through the courts.

The distinguishing mark of the child abuse crisis is that it is difficult to trace, involves all sorts of extra elements such as denial and cover up and its consequences are far deeper, more lasting and extensive for victims, their families, whole communities and the Church at large.

For victims and their families, the experience of abuse has been life arresting and life changing. But for many Catholics, the discovery of the depth and extent of the abuse, along with the managerial ineptitude with which the incidents and their victims have been handled, has also been arresting and life changing, affecting the confidence and trust they can maintain in the Church, its claims and its leadership.

It is small comfort to say that, when it was introduced in the 1990s, the Australian Church's Professional Standards Protocol was world's best practice. For example, when the US bishops eventually got around to doing something serious and comprehensive about their sex abuse problems in 2002, they invited the Australian bishops to contribute from their experience to the creation of a national protocol.

However, now there are serious questions about the quality of our processes, the competence of its administration, whether its requirements were adhered to and whether its localised management was conducted with the rigour needed.

Now the Royal Commission will scrutinise the Protocol and the other Church procedure introduced by Cardinal Pell when Archbishop of Melbourne, called the Melbourne Response. The Commission's job will be to see if they pass muster and their execution has been faithful.

Living in a pluralist democracy where the rule of law prevails, the Australian Church will have the benefit of external intervention and evaluation by outsiders. Only good can come of that.

Both of the Protocols, and now the Royal Commission and several other enquiries in various States, address two other questions that we as a community of faith need to respond to:

1. Pastoral care for the victims and their families; and
2. Pastoral care for those Catholics disillusioned by what has been revealed and discouraged in a faith journey as part of the Catholic community

The answer to the first question plainly requires a comprehensive, personalised and enduring commitment of resources and personnel. It is a response to be made by those who control the Church's resources on our behalf.

The answer to the second question—how to address the discouragement, dismay and feeling of disappointment and alienation felt by many Catholics—is more varied and complex and much harder to propose solutions to.

But I would like to face that challenge and present to you what I believe is the first requirement when facing something of these proportions.

And it's not as though we are inexperienced in doing this. In one way or another, we humans are doing it all the time and every day.

What we are in the midst of is a traumatic change. Trauma is something anyone can identify as part of their own experience of life and the observant among us can recognise the response to trauma as either successful or unsuccessful in others.

I work daily in an industry that catalogues trauma—mass communications media—where the long held view of successful editors is 'you've got to make them sigh or make them cry'. And there are whole industries devoted to helping people cope with trauma.

In the 1990s, I worked with a group to raise money for an innovative project generated by Sydney's Matt Talbot Hostel. It was a novel program developed first in the United States for alcoholic street people that was based on teaching people to read and then discover good reading. The aim of the exercise was to give the subjects of the program the language and structure to tell their own story by reading good stories produced by great writers.

As part of the fundraising, we held many events graced by the presence and patronage of the NSW Governor, Professor Marie Bashir.

Gracious and courteous as Her Excellency is, the Governor knows more than her prayers. She is an extensively experienced psychiatrist and has had a great deal to do with homeless, itinerant alcoholics. The clientele of the Matt Talbot Hostel has changed since she worked in the inner city of Sydney. It now deals with more drug abusing and clinically disturbed people than when Professor Bashir was at work professionally, in the 1960s and 1970s. Many people who ended up at the Talbot in those days would today be diagnosed as suffering from post-traumatic stress syndrome connected to experiences in World War II and the Korean and Vietnam Wars.

Professor Bashir would refer to such people as ones who had learnt to self-medicate their condition. Trauma, unlike appendicitis, is not something that announces its arrival with acute pain. Trauma, like depression, creeps up on you and it's not till you're well into it that you even recognise the change in yourself. If you do recognise it and the condition is not too far advanced and you have the courage to face it, the first thing to do is seek help.

That assistance may entail medication but sooner or later it will lead back to where Sigmund Freud started—telling your story. Therapeutic counselling—from the free association championed by Dr Freud to all the therapies flowing from or created in contrast to his work—depend on one thing: narrative.

Which brings us back to the insight proposed for the program at the Matt Talbot Hostel.

Telling our story and owning our history is the first step to getting hold of what's dominating and controlling us. How do we know what we mean till we hear what we say?

Hearing the story—our own or listening to others'—has colossal implications for us as individuals and also as communities. Not being listened to or not listening to what our hearts and bodies are saying to us is as silly and destructive as being told there are things we aren't allowed to discuss. And that, as a practice, has a habit of turning up as the directive of all threatened authoritarian regimes, even at various stages in the life of the Church. It always fails as a strategy by the potentates.

I say this not to distract from any duty owed in compassion and justice to the trigger for this crisis—the victims of sexual abuse at the hands of Catholic ministers.

I say it simply because what I want to do is address something that hasn't been addressed or addressed adequately—the collateral damage to others also traumatised by what they see happening in a community that they have come to trust, a community to which a quarter of the children under 18 in Australia are entrusted for their education, a community where despite falling Mass attendance there is no slackening in the desire of adults to identify with the Catholic faith by having their children baptised into it or indeed to have adults actually joining it.

Just as I find it clarifying to name sex abusers as psychopathic criminals (and I think a great deal of good would be done if those convicted of these offences were seen as sick people who have broken the law), so also I think it would be helpful to nominate our time in the Church as one where, among other things, we have to live with and treat a trauma that impacts variously on individuals but casts its shadow over us all.

I would like now to turn to the narrative. What we need to develop as a community of believers with the challenge to follow Jesus is this: we need an account of our experience that renders our journey meaningful and the choices we make about our faith plausible.

Clearly then what we need is something to say about our shared experience and about our personal journey to discover light, understanding and peace.

Starting with the broader canvas—the life we share together in the community of faith—let's see it as it is. Our society is being impacted by changes that are occurring at an accelerating rate. In just 40 years, the life of Australians has changed beyond imagining and will continue to do so. The economy has moved to being a substantially service based activity away from agriculture and manufacturing, driven by changes in communications and transport. Australians are part of a world community now enjoying significantly enhanced levels of wealth, education, knowledge of people and places beyond our vast island continent; a transformation in the lives of women, engagements between men and women and people of the same gender; and being a Catholic is now quite different from what it was two generations ago.

Let's take it for granted that the fact of profound and extensive change is our context. Change of course means not only the presentation of an array of new options to choose from. It also means the end of so much that was taken for granted—about statuses, practices, expectations of behaviours and so much more. In a word, change also means death and the associated grief at losing something treasured and bewilderment about future prospects.

And for us Catholics, the last two generations have experienced a period of astonishing change in the practices, statuses, procedures and focus of our faith to a degree not witnessed in half a millennium. And what that change has done and means is rich and complex to say the least. As the Sydney priest, Edmund Campion, once cryptically observed, when the priest turned to face the people for the celebration of Mass, a lot more changed that the angle of his gaze.

Add to this context, the revelation of a reality that has been occurring at the same time—the reality of sexual abuse. This is something that was once known to a few and is now common knowledge to all. It is something that undermines the credibility of claims about faith as a transformative force. In other words, the reach of the changes having an impact on our faith community is profound. They go to the core of what Catholicism has been for so many for so long—a reassuring oasis in the midst of life's deserts, a reliable structure which, if never exactly avant garde, was at least reliable and trustworthy and able to provide the support and sustenance we need—support as much given directly by God as carried by the strength and constancy of relationships and found in the Catholic community.

It is important to realise that the changes that swirl in us and around us are not necessarily going to overwhelm us. They can be managed constructively or, if ignored or denied, end in destructive outcomes.

The American Benedictine Sister Joan Chittister perceptively observed recently in the National Catholic Reporter (Nov 16, 2012):

> It is possible to repress change temporarily—to slow change, to resist change, to deny change—but it is impossible to stop a change whose time has come. It is impossible to ignore change once it has begun to well up through the cracks in the cement of a society, however rigid the barriers to it.
>
> Repressed, people will resist. Ignored, people will remove themselves from an arthritic society. Unheard and unheeded, blocked and obstructed, the seed of a new idea simply grows

like ground pine until the ideas break out everywhere and an evolution that could have been handled by a process of peaceful reform gives away to unmanageable revolution. Ask the King and Queen of France.

Lest we fall into the trap that snared the King and Queen of France, we need to manage the change in so far as it is in our hands to do so. And it's my contention that the best way to do that at this stage is to name the phenomenon we are experiencing and build a narrative from there.

I've mentioned several times already in this paper that what we are experiencing collectively is trauma. It is partly triggered by shock and partly conditioned by witnessing at a local and global level the sheer ineptitude of some key leaders of our faith community who see and live in a different world to the one that most of us do, articulate a meaning that is far from adequate in explaining the data and whose ears seem closed to what many are saying.

It approaches a sort of socialised schizophrenia. Something is dying or is already dead and no one wants to have a funeral.

I'm struck by the parallels between our circumstances and responses to them and what Elizabeth Kubler-Ross published many years ago in her ground-breaking study of the process and stages of dying.

Kubler-Ross found that when presented with the results of a biopsy, a diagnosis of a lethal condition or a prognosis about a likely death, patients characteristically receive the information and file it under 'F' for forget. Denial of a terrifying piece of information is the first stage in Kubler-Ross's process.

Denial, that very familiar human response that allows us all to get out of bed each day in defiance of all that may and does befall us on any day, is a rich gift. Without it, we would be paralysed by anxiety. With it for too long, we go loopy. And whole cultures, even Empires, have practised it to excess only to see their whole world come tumbling down.

And that's what happens: we collapse under the weight of the facts—the unpleasant and the unpalatable eventually dawn and their light can't be escaped. And what it provokes is the next stage in Kubler Ross's process—anger. Why me? Why now? What about my plans? I don't deserve this etc, etc.

Anger fizzles out. We can't maintain the rage. I say to myself that this is no way to live what's left of life. So I enter the third stage of dealing with death. I start bargaining: if only I do this, I'll get that result; if only God permits this, I will go gracefully; etc, etc .

But we don't get the desired result. And then we become self-accusing: what a worthless dill I am to end up like this! All the symptoms of natural depression are evident. Life loses any interest; even gestures of encouragement and support are felt to be at best condescension and at times even intimidating. The world narrows down to me and my woes. And so the fourth phase in the Kubler Ross stages gets its run: depression.

But that doesn't last. Time and the relentless process eventually demonstrate the futility of blaming ourselves for something that has happened to us. Why futile? Because the dying person isn't getting the result he or she is wanting and the reality of what's going on dawns.

What dawns? Eventually recognition of what's going on comes for the dying person and acceptance of what's happening can follow. Letting go of something that is completely out of your hands can bring the peace that ends the struggle.

Typologies such as Kubler-Ross presents are abstractions. They cannot represent reality in all its mixed confusion. And as with all typologies, the Kubler Ross description of death and dying can in fact be found in all or most of its phases in a dying person at the same time. One definitive state isn't reached till the heart stops beating.

So it's smart to be flexible in using such an analytic tool. And it's wise to be careful in applying it to other circumstances in life apart from the process of dying.

But these phases and stages do have a resonance with the way we humans handle 'limit conditions'—death most obviously, but also other circumstances that can be described as traumatic such as getting the sack, the split of a marriage, the death of someone intimately close or the realisation at last that you have been completely misled and even lied to.

Just as I think it's not only accurate but healthy to name sexual abusers as psychopathic criminals, I also think it's accurate and healthy to call this time in the Church a trauma.

And naming it as a trauma, I think you can imagine what I'm going to say next: all manner of responses to it from denial to peaceful and mature acceptance, including anger, depression and bargaining, are evident in the Church at the moment. And such mood swings and dispositions are evident also in response to the very plain efforts throughout the world by many senior figures in the Catholic Church to turn the clock back, refuse to listen to anyone but their inner circle and dismiss criticism as the posturing of disloyal dissidents.

In brief, it's a mess and almost anything from total collapse and effective disappearance to revitalising and refreshing renewal can come from these circumstances.

I'm no specialist on death and dying. I prefer to focus on the living. So what I have to say is no expert diagnosis. Still my bush priest's pastoral instinct suggests to me that, in Australia, a lot of Catholics are somewhere between anger and depression. At times you hear people who may be into the bargaining stage when the 'if only' arguments are rehearsed—if only we had women in ministry, if only the unsustainability of mandatory clerical celibacy was seen and acted on and so on. But in general, I find it's anger at being misled or witnessing the mismanagement of a community they love or the equivalent of depression that is expressed in a shrug of the shoulders and the fatalistic belief that nothing can be done.

Clearly, for pastoral care to be effective, this condition needs to be addressed at a number of levels. Some time ago, the American sociologist, Peter Berger, noted that most of the notions that hold our societies together—democracy, the law, religion, for example—are abstractions and only become effective when intermediate structures are established to make them work—parliamentary or congressional processes, courts, Church communities with religious missions and ceremonies for people to enact and share. Catholicism is particularly weak in the creation and management of its intermediate structures. What ones that do exist are subject to a completely dysfunctional form of governance discarded by everyone in the world but the North Koreans and the Saudi Arabians: a lifelong absolute monarchy that may not be perpetuated by inheritance but certainly fulfils the old joke about priests—the only male celibate group able to reproduce itself. And beneath the lifelong, absolute and male monarchy is a support structure of clerics and bishops.

A lot of work—no more than suggested at Vatican 2—needs to be done on effective intermediate structures for such a diverse, multicultural multinational as the Latin Rite of the Catholic Church. Its current structures are not the fruit of revelation and as they stand—a centralising absolute monarchy—are plainly incapable of meeting the governance challenge of this time.

But I will leave later speakers in this Camino series to address that question. What I want to focus on now is more something we can address for ourselves: how do we as followers of Jesus respond to this time when the Church appears by turn to be puzzling, chaotic, scandalous and at times irrelevant to the lives we lead? The question I am asking is what is the cost of discipleship now?

This time in the Church in Australia is tragic. The unhelpful intervention by Cardinal Pell on this subject—the Catholics 'aren't the only cab on the rank'—have highlighted an all too familiar pattern of aggressive defensiveness that generated plenty of heat, lots of 'I told you so' observations from his critics and no advance in understanding this time in the Church as one of unmatched shame.

Fortunately, other more mature voices among the bishops—and not just retired ones who can't be harassed by the Vatican—have weighed in with the appropriate contrition and compassion which is all that should be displayed as the catastrophe of child abuse and the incompetent and possibly criminal response to it by some generations of church leadership is documented.

While countless Catholics, me among them, feel nothing but shame and sorrow at this unfolding—both the abuse of victims and its insensitive and selfish handling by authorities in dioceses and religious congregations—it is far from clear how best an ordinary Catholic can and should respond to this spectacle of culpability in the Church.

Many I have talked to in recent months are dismayed and shocked, questioning why they should bother to ever identify themselves as Catholics again. Christina Keneally has recently posed in Eureka Street the dilemma that faces informed Catholics seeking to raise their children in the faith. Not a few of us in the full-time employment of the Church have found it hard even to imagine the next steps we should take.

May I make three suggestions?

First, from adolescence I have been guided by the advice of an old Jesuit who responded to my description of the pettiness, fear and cowardice of some members of the Jesuit community I was in at the time.

'You're a strange sort of Christian if you are overwhelmed by the scandalous deeds of others,' he told me. That brought me up short and still does.

He wasn't denying the dilapidated humanity, absence of faith and hope, and outright lovelessness in what I had told him. He just fronted me with the brutal reality everyone has to face at such a time. In a succinct way he was asking me: After such knowledge, what forgiveness?

And that leads to the second response I would propose. The only reason Christians can look on human depravity in all its horror and not succumb before it is this: our faith is in a crucified Lord. Without it, in the face of tragedy we would be well advised to agree that nihilism is the only adequate way of thinking about and responding to our own and others' evil.

Jesus died a shameful death and at times in our lives, in private and sometimes in shared ways, we do too.

The clear evidence of depravity in the Church should really only surprise the naive. But whether we are naive or jaundiced or just bewildered, each of us has to reckon with our experience, absorb a little or a lot of pain and pray in our powerlessness for the transforming power of God to do what we can't do ourselves. From the first page of the Old Testament, the God proclaimed is one who makes something out of nothing.

And the black hole that is the horror of sex abuse, hidden In the Church for so long, is a 'nothing', an abyss of darkness into which we stare, undermining any confidence we might have had in declarations of anyone's good intentions.

The third suggestion I would like to make is that we learn from something St Ignatius Loyola wisely perceived and warmly encouraged us to adopt.

Some of you may be familiar with what is the most portable part of his spiritual legacy that goes by the name of the Examen or the examination of conscience. It starts with a prayer of gratitude and then looks for the light and darkness in one's experience in the preceding hours, all with a view to being led by the Spirit through sometimes painful and sometimes delightful experience. Followers of Ignatius' spiritual practice may do this several times a day for five to fifteen minutes.

It is rendered more intelligibly to us in this age as the examination of consciousness. Really what it boils down to is a reading of the mood swings we go through and how they can lead us to or away from God, how we can grow deeper in our faith and love or just bubble away at a superficial level perpetually.

For Ignatius, one unmistakable mood that can swamp us and, if we let it go unexamined and unchecked, can shield us from the face of God is the common experience of disappointment and discouragement.

This tragic time in the Church is one of great disillusionment and many reflect to me all the signs of discouragement. People feel let down and powerless to alter a situation they care about deeply but feel out of their depth to influence in any constructive way.

It's a common mood, one we all know in our families and with those we love as we watch them destroy themselves and it can paralyse us as we stand by looking for something to do in response but knowing what's needed is beyond our resources. It eats away at us and we end up blaming ourselves and, at times, becoming part of the problem we are looking to fix.

Ignatius labelled this dark mood of discouragement as just one more instance of desolation—an experience of God's absence. His antidote was to name it as the darkness it is but he also suggested that it is the shadow side of God's presence. It offers in a new and unexpected way an opportunity to grow. How? Ignatius encourages his followers to make the surrender of love and yield patiently to God till the darkness lifts, confident that the God who stirred the desire which has been disappointed will see to its mysterious transformation in ways we could never ask for or imagine.

Our time is one of deep disappointment, of despondency and desolation. Of course it will pass. But persevered through in faith, it can enrich you and me and be the midwife of the transformation desired.

So where does this leave us personally and spiritually? I am pleased to report that being a child on the 1950s, I got to watch a lot of TV in the 1960s, especially the vintage comedy of the 1930s and 1940s that was replayed in black and white. One particular duo that always got a laugh in my childhood was the sophisticated slapstick of Laurel and Hardy. Invariably, the overbearing and thinly disguised contempt that Oliver Hardy had for the bumbling and inept Stan Laurel would end Ollie up with having to carry the can and blaming Stan. It may well have been (and often was) a caper that Ollie initiated. But Stan had to be blamed. And he always was, with Ollie saying 'Well it's a fine mess you've got me into this time Stanley'.

And of this time, I think we can all agree that we are in a mess.

In the Spiritual Exercises, St Ignatius, in different meditations, especially in the Second Week, invites the retreatant to consider and contemplate how God is 'labouring' away in the world, refusing to be frustrated by the incompetence and evil worked by us self-interested and often ignorant humans. This always grabs my imagination especially in the various holes I've found myself in life.

It is a hope filled assertion that more is at play than can be beheld by the naked eye, that even when all seems lost, the last word hasn't been uttered.

Let me conclude by saying that change never comes to everyone at once. It is often been said it takes 100 years for a Council of the Church to be received. We are only halfway down the Vatican II track.

Whether we grow stronger and deeper in our faith through the shocks and traumas we experience, it is always God who has the initiative. And, despite our obstinacy, that's what we wait for.

Forum for Theology in the World Vol 2 No 1/2015

Our Church Further Down the Track

Christopher Geraghty

When I take time out of a busy life to reflect on our Catholic Church, I like to pause and call to mind the untidy mob wandering into St Vincent's Redfern for the 10 o'clock Mass on Sunday, talking loudly out of turn, greeting Father Ted Kennedy in the middle of his homily, kissing him affectionately on the cheek, some unsteady on their feet—the poor, the lost, the disoriented, the weak and the derelict. 'Where two or three are gathered together in my name . . .' As I observed, and participated in the Redfern liturgy, I used to smile quietly to myself as I imagined what was happening just a few miles away, on the edge of Hyde Park, at the cathedral. Glorious, polyphonic choral hymns haunting the vast upper spaces, solemn processions of important men in their ceremonial gear, scented smoke wafting through the congregation. Two different Catholic celebrations glorifying God and struggling to survive in the modern world.

However much we like to think that our Church is well-ordered, uniformed and neatly presented on the public arena, ruled from Rome and standing to attention, in reality God's people is more like a multitudinous rabble, a mob of unruly people—a few rich members (some extremely generous; too many with short arms and deep pockets), but most members surviving in poverty in the rat-holes and on the rubbish heaps of the world; men and women of all different sexual and political persuasions; people with serious psychological and psychiatric conditions and none; gifted poets and mystics; eminent theologians and scientists; faceless men and women of truly humbling generosity; silent witnesses to gospel values; liars, cheats and sexual deviants; saints and sinners; some of us putting their faith in trivial rituals, novenas, rapid-fire prayer formulas and pagan superstitious practices; financial traders driving Ferraris and sun-burnt farmers on rusty tractors; the educated and the ignorant—every member with his or her own personal beliefs and prejudices, his habits, her array of attitudes, their own private lives, failures and successes, prelates and paupers, pimps and prostitutes as well as members of St Vincent de Paul and the Legion of Mary, millions and millions of us—some who truly, deeply believe, some who want to believe, others who pretend to believe and some with no faith at all. Whatever you think of the Vatican and its bloodless bureaucrats, our Catholic Church is truly catholic, and the vast majority of its many millions of members live a long way from Rome.

In December 2012, Andrew West of the Australian ABC's Radio National wrote a piece for the *Sydney Morning Herald* in which he observed that, despite the ugly scandals surrounding the Catholic Church and her clergy, despite the intellectual and cultural dominance of secularism, agnosticism and atheism, our churches and other faith communities remain the strongest centres of public good in our society.

It is important to take note of this fact here at the beginning of my essay on the future of the Catholic Church. There are features of our Church which we must treasure and support. From her early days, and now in recent times, she has preached and practised a glorious social Gospel of care, justice, equality and civic fairness. Protection of workers through the power of trade unions. Just wages. Dignified respect for every human being. Education for all, and especially for girls. Nursing the sick, feeding the hungry, advocating for the poor, caring for the elderly. Each parish and local community can pride itself on a team of volunteer labourers and a disproportionate number of people employed in the caring professions.

Among church people

> You will also find . . . political views that are, on the whole, more left-wing, and education levels that are higher than those of the broader community.

Like other members of the community who maintain a spiritual and religious life, we Catholics are deeply involved in working and caring for others—St Vincent de Paul, World Vision or Caritas, Meals on Wheels, Amnesty International, active members of political parties, protest groups, or refugee and asylum seekers support organisations,

Aboriginal rights. We have much to be proud of and an impressive record to preserve—and while we can level serious criticisms at our organisation, we should never forget our heritage.

And now, at long last, we have a leader who promises to return our vast organisation to the values of Jesus, the values on which it was founded. The signs are encouraging. Pope Francis wants a simpler Church which speaks to the people and to the world and which allows, perhaps even encourages, the people and the world to speak to her—one in which the poor are preferred and given pride of place.

In his Second Vatican Council journal, Yves Congar recorded that on Tuesday 23 October 1962, in preparation for the council, he had told Mgr Leon-Arthur Elchinger, co-adjutor bishop in the Diocese of Strasbourg where he was living, that people were expecting the Council to address the questions of how to simplify Church life as well as how to prioritise the evangelical principle of poverty. He made three suggestions:

1. The council had to renounce its *Seigneurial* culture, cease to act as lord and master, to dominate and control, and surrender all its pretentions of temporal prestige.
2. The council should create real contact with people so that priests and members of the hierarchy are not cut off from them—in other words, solve the perennial problem of clericalism.
3. The Church must be, and must appear to be much more—the Church of the Poor.[1]

On Saturday 10 March 1962, Congar was travelling home to Strasbourg from Rome where, on that same day he had lunched with Cardinal Ottaviani and a number of bishops. He had spent time discussing part of a draft of the Constitution on the Church, more particularly on the nature of the Church, with Fr Tromp SJ, a Roman and influential Jesuit theologian in the old, close-minded scholastic mould. He was travelling by train from Como with a group of Italian men who were leaving their families in Italy in search of work in Germany and Holland.

---

1. Yves Congar, *My Journal of the Council*, translated by Mary John Ronayne OP and Mary Cecily Boulding OP (Adelaide: ATF Press, 2012), 115.

> What likeable people they were! In their bread (large, coarse, 'ordinary' bread) they ate sausage, cheese, bananas, enough to keep me going for a full two days. They are cheerful, they laugh at everything. They show me photos of their wives and children.

Then he adds a simple but sad observation:

> What a dose of true uncomplicated humanity. How far removed from our Roman and clerical concerns![2]

This was a constant Congar complaint which he recorded in his journal—that the Roman Curia was focused on itself, on preserving its own position and buttressing the absolute power of the Papacy, that its functionaries were 'old bachelors', out of step with ordinary men and women. He frequently spelt out the cruel distinction between the Ecclesia, the Church, the real Church on the one hand, and the Curia in Rome—two totally different institutions.

On 17 April, 2010 in *The New York Times* Nicholas Kirstof wrote of the great divide between Rome and the Curia on the one hand, and the real Church on the other:

> In my travels around the world, I encounter two Catholic Churches. One is the rigid all-male Vatican hierarchy that seems out of touch when it bans condoms even among married couples where one partner is HIV positive. To me at least, this church—obsessed with dogma and rules and distracted from social justice—is a modern echo of the Pharisees whom Jesus criticised.

> Yet there's another Catholic Church as well, one I admire intensely. This is the grass-roots Catholic Church that does far more good in the world than it ever gets credit for. This is the church that supports extraordinary aid organisations like Catholic Relief Services and Caritas, saving lives every day, and that operates superb schools that provide needy children an escalator out of poverty.

> This is the church of the nuns and priests in Congo, toiling in obscurity to feed and educate children. This is the church of the Brazilian priest fighting AIDS who told me that if he

---

2. Yves Congar, *My Journal of the Council*, 79.

> were pope, he would build a condom factory in the Vatican to save lives.
>
> This is the church of the Maryknoll Sisters in Central America and the Cabrini Sisters in Africa. There's a stereotype of nuns as stodgy Victorian traditionalists. I learned otherwise while hanging on for my life in a passenger seat as an American nun with a lead foot drove her jeep over ruts and through a creek in Swaziland to visit AIDS orphans. After a number of encounters like that, I've come to believe that the very coolest people in the world today may be nuns.
>
> So when you read about the scandals, remember that the Vatican is not the same as the Catholic Church. Ordinary lepers, prostitutes and slum-dwellers may never see a cardinal, but they daily encounter a truly noble Catholic Church in the form of priests, nuns and lay workers toiling to make a difference.

Between the second and third sessions of the Council, Congar was busy drafting and redrafting various documents, answering his mail, delivering lectures to seminarians in Milan, furthering the cause closest to his heart—the communion of all Christians and developing an ecclesiology based on Communion. In the course of his travels, he found himself in Turin dining with Count Dal Verme, an old Italian soldier aged ninety-one whose family was a member of the ancient nobility of Italy.

> What a strange milieu is this milieu of ancient nobility (the family has been known in Milan since the twelfth century) that still has something of a fortune: others no longer have anything, and live in two or three rooms, strangers to the modern world. These are VERY cultivated people, but I was conscious of how artificial, empty and unreal was the set-up of drawing rooms hung with old paintings, of domestic servants in white gloves etc. It is a bit like the set-up on the Vatican . . .[3]

There's the Church—and then—there's the Church.

---

3. Yves Congar, *My Journal of the Council*, 490.

In his journal, Congar constantly returned to the stark contrast between the two ecclesiologies which were on show daily at the Council—two different images of the Church being projected on the global screen.

> The Roman, curial Church, the ultramontane Church gomflated with pomp and superiority, forever concerned with its dignity and status, super-dogmatic, assertive, isolated, reactionary and authoritarian. This Church revolves around the pope who is carried in procession on the shoulders of his attendants, on the papal sedia, fanned by large ostrich feathers and encased in clouds of incense. This Church embarrassed Congar. He said that the Gospel was present in the Church, but as a prisoner.
>
> The other Church is the real one—the People of God, inclusive, engaged in the world, the protector and champion of the poor, based on the values and principles of Jesus as set out in the Gospels, with a humble pope at the head, surrounded and assisted by a college of bishops.

He observed:

> It must be acknowledged that, since the beginning (of the Council), throughout the whole preparatory period, and since the opening of the Council, there has been an on-going conflict between the *Ecclesia* and the Curia. The further I go, the more it appears to me that the purely Italian structure of the Roman organisms and of the Roman ideology is the tumour that needs to be cut away. Ultramontanism as an ideology certainly exists. And it is very close to being a heresy![4]

Some modern western gurus (philosophers, poets, sociologists) earn fat fees advising giant institutions (banks, government bureaucracies, hospitals, law firms, insurance companies) on how the members of the board and their CEOs can expect their organisation to look and function in twenty or fifty years. They use their expertise and their imagination, thinking outside the square, to devise scenarios as to what a particular institution might look like in the future; identifying the problems and challenges which are likely to emerge; imagining new, radical inventions and discoveries which might change the way

---

4. Yves Congar, *My Journal of the Council*, 425.

we think, or do business, or travel; listing future stressors and needs which must be considered; describing future community attitudes to be dealt with, changing worldviews which might put pressure on the organisation or alternatively, which might provide a distinct advantage to the company. These gurus, shamans or charlatans, attempt to define what we would like our world to be like in fifty years time, where we want it to go and what we should do now to encourage our world to proceed in a particular direction, to be ready for whatever might come. These secular soothsayers function on the edge of business and management schools, in medical and law faculties, governmental and planning agencies. They simply assume that the world of the future is not going to be like it is now and that in all likelihood it will be radically different, perhaps unrecognisable. Smart phones, global warming, cosmetic surgery, population explosions, water wars, cyberspace travel and cosmic weaponry—and other factors at present beyond our imagining. These experts speak of preparing us for change, educating us to deal with uncertainty and cognitive dissonance, to become adaptable in the way we live, in the way we think.

As far as I can see, our ecclesial institution (the local version, for example in Sydney, the national version, and especially the global version centralised in the Vatican) is far from engaged in this type of organisational or personnel planning. Instead, we are faced with three unsatisfactory ecclesiastical strategies.

1. Try to shut down all attempts at renewal and change, and recapture the past, recreate the Church before Vatican II, before the 60's, before Vatican I and return the Church to at least the time of Pius IX, if not to a time before the French Revolution.
2. Close the draw-bridge, fill the moat, release the crocodiles and hold the fort as long as necessary. The building is crumbling, the occupants are leaving, but a faithful rump will remain and build again, in the old style.
3. Let the pendulum swing. There is an ebb and flow in the life of society, and in the Church. We've been through bad times before. It's bad again now, but it'll change. We must trust in a providential God. Jesus assured us that all would be well. Our Church as we know it is protected by God and will never fail.

But who in the name of God is looking to our Church further down the track—not to the end of the world, or to the promised golden millennium, but to the situation for Christians and their communities in fifty years time, for our children and their children? That's what leaders are supposed to do—not hanker after past glories, often imaginary—not try to recapture and recycle the past. A wise and prudent man looks to the future. As an act of ordinary bloody common sense, Jesus read the signs of the times, and encouraged his followers to do the same. He advised them to look to the future, to be ready to move, to be on guard to seize the moment. He told the story of the ten virgins—five prudent, and five stupid and dull.

> When it is evening, you say, 'It will be fair weather; for the sky is red.' And in the morning, 'It will be stormy today, for the sky is red and threatening.' You know how to interpret the appearance of the sky, but you cannot interpret the signs of the times.[5]
>
> Look at the fig tree, and all the trees; as soon as they come out in leaf, you see for yourselves and know that the summer is already near. So also, when you see these things taking place, you know that the kingdom of God is near.[6]

It is the bleeding obvious. Read the signs of the times. Look up. Look out. Look around. Use your common sense. We should not spend our lives with our eyes closed and our ears blocked. We are meant to look to the future and plan. Change is part of living. Change is inevitable. We either go with the flow, join in it, welcome and accept it, participate and try in our way to control it and benefit from it, or we survive in the shadows, on the fringe of society, in the ghettos. At the moment, the signs are good. The new pope has a mammoth job, but during these early days and months he has been able to put smiles on the faces of his people and furrows in the brows of his bureaucrats. The Catholic world stands ready to embrace the world and the future with Francis.

So, let's have a look around and listen to the murmurings of our era. As Catholics, we are confronted with two basic questions—

---

5. Mt 16:2–3.
6. Luke 21:29.

1. The *historical* question—what kind of Church have we been getting?
2. The *future* question—what kind of Church do we want?

What kind of Church have we been getting?
I don't really want to go there. We can all answer the question for ourselves, and there are many positions on a wide spectrum of opinion. You might find my analysis too bleak.

As I see it now at the end of my life, the kind of Church the Vatican and her episcopal appointees have been in the process of delivering, in the West at least, is riddled with a spray of deep-rooted scandals—a significant number of clergy who are criminals, and of high-ranking superiors who, in the name of Jesus and to protect his Church's reputation, have been moving them around, protecting them from exposure and from the short arm of the law. We have had an excessively centralised Church which is choking the breath out of small, local communities. We have been ruled by elderly men who have persisted in dressing up like chooks in funny feathers. Theologians, and others with a vision and a bag of pretty harmless ideas, until recently have been under constant threat of persecution. The dictates of natural justice are for others to observe and for the Church to preach, but not apply to its dealings with its own. Letters of complaint have been ignored. The administration has been strictly controlled by rules and oaths of secrecy. Membership has been growing old. People have been drifting away. The leaders have been carefully chosen after they have proved themselves to be excessively trustworthy and sycophantic— reactionary, paternalistic and authoritarian—all men. They have not been listening to, or communicating with our modern world. The dead hand of clericalism, with its club rules, its spin, its closed ranks, its power structures have been sapping the life and energy out of the Christian community. Tired old formulas have constituted the test of orthodoxy and acceptance. Too much dogma. Too much wealth. Too many old men. Rigid. Dogmatic. Negative. Reactionary. Keen supporters of secular society's establishment, based on principles and attitudes inimical to the Gospel—power, privilege, suppression, secrecy, pomp and greed. Against everything, and with no real solutions to any of the world's problems—poverty, over-population, war, violence, corruption. Basically irrelevant. As I said, I don't want to go there. Pope Francis is giving hope to the world and to us, of radical change. The signs are good, but as you see, I think the task is immense.

When you are on the inside, it's hard to see the group to whom you belong as others see it. But we all have to try, because those others out there are our brothers. They are the reason why Jesus walked the earth and suffered, and why our Church exists.

The kind of Church we want, the kind of Church I would like to see is more open, more inclusive, more local, decentralised, less legalistic, more pastoral, more women-friendly—a community which can laugh and dance, which sings joyfully and celebrates, which can humbly admit sinfulness and seek forgiveness, one which champions the cause of the poor, of prisoners, the blind, refugees and the disabled. I want a Church which is not frightened of ideas but which encourages its prophets and thinkers, one which searches and struggles to talk to and communicate with the world, not one constipated by wealth, property, dogma, rituals, power and status. Out there in the marketplace rather than in the sacristy, challenging secular authority, not sleeping with it, preaching the simple message of the Word of God rather than defending the indefensible. I want the life and the belief system of my Church to be much simpler and more in tune with the style, the life and message of Jesus—and I want it to show a preference for the poor.

Our subversive memory

The history of the Church, in its simplest form, is the story of a community's faith-experience, down though the ages, of a young man whom his village parents had named 'Jesus'. He had been born in poverty to a young girl called Mary, married to a carpenter from Nazareth – Palestine's Mt Druitt. We know almost nothing of the story of this man before the age of about thirty when he appeared out of the wilderness, on a small stage, in a distant corner of the Roman Empire. For a short time, at the most two or three years, he was a itinerant storyteller and preacher, a wonder-worker who travelled around, in and out of towns and villages, with a band of mates, some faithful women friends, and further back, a crowd of occasional sympathetic and hostile followers. He had attitude. He did not fit in. A loner. Misunderstood. He refused to show submissive servile respect for the many petty laws and regulations of the society, or for its religious leaders. Eventually he proved to be such a threat to the establishment, such a challenge to religious institutional order and good government, to authority and those in power, that the authorities crucified him, and his friends buried his body in a stranger's tomb.

After his barbaric death, Jesus' followers began to experience his presence among them, often in little, nervous gatherings. At first, these men and women who had lived with him for a few years, for some strange reason, did not seem to recognise him, though gradually they came to accept him as strangely present to them, not as he had once been, but in a new, mysterious way. They used to meet together. They prayed. They meditated and reflected on the experience they had shared, living with Jesus, listening to him, watching him as they travelled around. They began to tell stories about him and to repeat, as far as they could remember them, his words, his parables, his sayings and his vision of a strange kingdom. Gradually they began to record their memory of the events of his life and death, his stories and advice, and to puzzle over the meaning Jesus had for them. They began to interpret this seminal Jesus-event and to search for ways of speaking about his birth and his appearance in the world, his mission, his vision, his death and his strange appearances among them after his death.

All this did not occur in a vacuum. Jesus was a Jew. His mother and her partner were Jews, and his mates and his women friends, his other followers and his enemies. They all belonged to a people who traced their proud ancestry back to Moses, to Abraham and to a mythological figure they called Adam. They had a literature, a culture, a heritage which they all shared. So when his friends began to reflect about their experience of Jesus, to talk among themselves and to others about him and their short life together, they naturally drew on a rich reservoir of images, metaphors, heroic figures and significant events in order to communicate what Jesus meant to them. They spoke of him as the suffering servant, the Emmanuel, the Lamb of God, the son of man, the messiah, the saviour, the perfect sacrificial victim, the high priest, God's prophet, a second Adam, a second Moses, a new lawgiver. A Christian way of thinking was gradually emerging, and a literature recorded in the language of the country—in Aramaic and a form of Greek as used by the Jewish people. These followers fashioned their community gatherings on their experience of the Jewish community gatherings for worship and prayer—the synagogue, the Passover feast, the Sabbath meal and initiation ceremonies. The early Christian liturgy developed on the model of Jewish ritual and ceremonial.

The primitive Church had to organise herself, especially after the penny dropped and the members began to realise that the world was not going to end tomorrow, that Christ was not going to appear in the heavens immediately. They had to consolidate the movement, create structures, establish positions in the community and functions (replace an apostle, appoint deacons and deaconesses, give legitimacy to elders, overseers, prophets, teachers), develop sacraments and ceremonies (baptisms, ordinations, conferral of the Spirit, anointing) and agree on rules and regulations for proper behaviour and ways of dealing with bad behaviour. For the first few years or decades the Church was in the process of emerging out of the profound, daily experience of Jesus among them and no longer among them as he used to be. The followers were adapting to a new situation, gradually, naturally.

To begin with the Christian community's experience of Jesus was in deep dialogue with the Semitic-Jewish world—filtering, mediating, expressing and celebrating the faith experience in Jewish images, metaphors, stories, and in the Jewish language. But that could not, and did not last. The Church was receiving a dribble of converts from another world, from among the pagans. The message was proving attractive to others. Paul was preaching about Jesus to people who were not Jews. They could not be expected to understand and appreciate the culturally determined images, metaphors and narratives of the Jewish Christians. A critical decision had to be made whether, and under what conditions, to welcome these pagans. A meeting of the leaders was held in Jerusalem in about 50 AD to decide these troubling issues. The meeting proved turbulent. To begin with, there was not general agreement. The apostles were seeing things differently. Open, frank discussion. No punches were held back. In the life of the early Church, the question of pagan applicants was far more radical than the more recent questions about the third rite of penance, or celibacy, of welcoming gays to the altar. It went to the very heart of Christianity and the message. Did the Christian community have to exclude the unwashed mob and only welcome Jews, or was it destined to be open, to include the world? Well, Paul prevailed over Peter, the first pope, and the Church went on to flourish, in fact to become the established religion in the East and West for some centuries, and in the west until the enlightenment, the age of secularism and modernism.

Our Church in the west has enjoyed a privileged but dangerous status in society since the time of Constantine. In the early fourth century, the Emperor's policy was to unite the Church to the secular State by the closest possible ties.

But before Christianity became Constantine's established religion throughout the Roman Empire, if the Church wanted to survive and grow, she had to dialogue seriously with the big world around her. If she wanted to spread the message and share her experience of Jesus, she had to communicate with others, enter their world, talk their language, mould her customs, carefully select her images and metaphors to suit the people in the towns and villages, and be part of the culture, the world wherever she found herself.

To begin with she was a tiny religious movement in a Semitic culture trying to survive and establish herself both in the world of Judaism, which in turn was on the edge of the Roman Empire, and to some extent at least, under the Roman provincial authority. The Church's language was Aramaic, as was Jesus'. Her theology, her celebrations and liturgy were deeply influenced by Judaic figures, heroes, events, images, metaphors and practices. The Christian message had to have a language and a culture in which to live and grow.

Then, under the influence of Paul and others, the Church sought to spread the message and to share the experience with a wider world—Asia Minor, Greece, Malta, Rome and perhaps Spain. She needed a new language, new images, new metaphors, a new frame of references. She had to adapt and change. Greek became the language of choice. Plato, neo-Platonism, Stoicism, Gnosticism became the thought-worlds, the milieu in which the Christian communities functioned. We can see the change in the writings of Paul, John the Evangelist, Justin, Clement, Ignatius of Antioch, Irenaeus of Lyon—and the list goes on.

When the Church moved into a different milieu in and around Alexandria, this necessitated further adaptation—a new school of theology, a new way of interpreting the sacred books, new ways of talking about Jesus, and a new language with all that that entailed. The

Christian message spread to North Africa, where Latin was spoken by the educated, where Latin literature was read, where Berber tribes lived on the edge of towns and in desert areas, where there was a Roman emphasis on law, on the military, on order and discipline. We are in the world of Tertullian and Augustine.

Before the time of Constantine, our Church had had to come to terms with several vastly different cultures, and by necessity, her life and message passed through a number of radical mutations and transfigurations. Her transit had not been easy. She had encountered and negotiated many challenges. She had travelled over rough terrain until she hit the highway in the early fourth century, and in the west, until recently, she never looked back over her shoulder.

As we struggle to read the signs of the times in the twenty-first century and to realign our faith community with the modern world, the story of the entry of Christian adventurers into the foreign world of the Far East in the seventh century can be both instructive and liberating. From the beginning, the Christian interlopers (intruders, newcomers) seemed to understand that if they wanted to live and thrive in China, they would need to use a language which was familiar to the Chinese and which was underpinned by Taoist and Buddhist thought patterns. They seemed to accept that they had to meet the Chinese on their own ground and embrace the challenges of explaining the Christian experience of Jesus which was central to their faith so the message had to be presented in terms which would make sense to people living in a culture which was alien to the new arrivals.

The first missionary, Alopen, and his successors presented their Christian faith in the form of sutras—in discourses framed in a typically Buddhist style. These Christians accepted the Buddha as a source of spiritual insight and revelation, but nevertheless, one which called for further amplification. The teachings of the Buddha were seen as inspired by the Holy Spirit. Alopen and those who came after him wrote a series of Jesus Sutras, some doctrinal (the *Jesus Messiah Sutra, the Sutra on the Origin of Origins, the Sutra on the Almsgiving of the World-Honored One*) and some liturgical *(Da Qin Hymn of Perfection of the Three Majesties, the Sutra of Ultimate and Mysterious Happiness, Da Qin Hymn to the Transfiguration of the Great Holy One)*. These Jesus Sutra demonstrate an uncomplicated co-mingling of the Christian message and philosophy with Buddhist and Taoist thought, and while their efforts are lost in the mists, they disclose to us that in different times and in many parts of the world, Christianity has met the challenge of adapting to the culture of the times. The Christian community was inspired to seek and find new ways of communicating with a variety of cultures and peoples.

Since Constantine and until the present era, until about 1900 in the West (maybe a little earlier, but not much, maybe until the French Revolution), Christianity had been in the ascendency. The Church had enjoyed the privileges of power, influence and position, the protection of the State, because she was imbedded in Western culture and its institutions. During that time, and under the influence of power, the institution grew to be more and more entrenched in the secular life of the State, more imperial, more authoritarian, more centralised, more legalistic and dogmatic, and consequently less inclined to, less able to change with the times. While the secular world changed after the French Revolution, the Church tried hard to pretend that it was immutable, that somehow an unwillingness to change showed strength and a divine foundation.

There are some among us still who want to believe that the Church has always been the same, that the whole administrative structure and the sacramental system were instituted by Jesus, handed down from one generation to the next and entrusted to us in the modern world, unchanged. Not true. Not remotely true. Dogma, morals, liturgy, structures have changed and developed constantly from age to age, culture to culture, country to country. It's easy to believe that our world is safe because what we know and experience now is what every Christian has known and experienced down the centuries. Not true. There has always been, from the beginning, a dynamic and often disturbing dialogue between continuity and discontinuity, between harmony, discord and change. The Christian world of the Middle Ages was different, radically different from that of the first and second centuries. For example, the way the Church community has exercised its power to forgive sins and control moral behavior has changed radically over the centuries, and undoubtedly will change again.

By way of example as to how the Church world has changed and will continue to change, let us compare the contemporary role of women in the liturgy in the parish of North Sydney with the ecclesiastical world of the period from the fourth to the ninth centuries.

If you attend the Sunday Eucharist at St Mary's, you will see female acolytes in white albs, women gathering on the altar to distribute communion under both species, women readers and leaders, and women, young and pretty women, leading the singing. It wasn't always like that.

In 494 AD, for example, Pope Gelasius wrote to the bishops of Lucania—

> As we have learnt to our anger, such a contempt for the divine truths has set in that even women, it has been reported, serve at the holy altars. And everything that is exclusively entrusted to the service of men has been carried out by the sex that has no right to do it.[7]

Canon 44 of the Synod of Laodicea which was held in about 370 AD, stated that: Women are not allowed to approach the altar.[8]

The same position was taken at the Synod of Nimes in 394[9], the Synod of Nantes in 658[10] and the Synod of Aachen in 789 AD.[11]

---

7. Letter IX, Ch XXVI, PL vol 59 cols 48, 55–56.
8. Canons of the Synod of Laodicea, Joannes Dom Mansi, *Sacrorum Conciliorum nova et amplissma Collectio*, tome II, Antonius Zatta Venice, 1759, cols 563–604; Charles Joseph Héfélé, *Histoire des Conciles d'après les documents originaux*, tome 1, deuxiéme partie (Paris: Letouzey et Ané, 1907), 1020; 'The Synod of Laodicea', *Nicene and Post-Nicene Fathers*, Second Series, volume 14 (New York: Christian Literature Publishing Co, 1900), Canon 44.
9. Canon 2. *Illud aetiam a quibusdam suggestum est, ut contra apostolicam disciplinam incognito usque in hoc tempus in ministerium feminae nescio quo loco levviticum videantur adsumptae; quod quidem, quia indecens est, non admittit ecclesiastica disciplina; et contra rationem facta talis ordinatio distruatur: providendum, ne quis sibi hoc ultra praesumat* . 'It has also been suggested by some persons that, contrary to the apostolic church order,—unheard of until this time!—women have been admitted to the levitical [= *diaconal*] ministry. I don't know in what place. This, however, is something church order does not allow because it is indecent. And since such an ordination has been performed against reason, it should be undone. Moreover, steps should be taken to ensure no one else will anymore presume to do such a thing. Charles Joseph Hefele, *A History of the Councils of the Church: From the Original Documents*, vol II AD326–AD429, translated by Henry Nutcombe Oxenham (Wipf and Stock, 2007), Book VIII, sectiion 110, 402ff.
10. Joannes Dom Mansi, *Sacrorum Conciliorum nova et amplissima Collectio*, tome XVIII, Antonius Zatta, Venice, 1773, Canon III, 167.
11. Monumenta Germaniae Historica (MGH), Legum Sectio II, *Capitularia regum Francorum*, tome I, edited by A Boretius, Ch 22, Admonitio Generalis, 23 Martio

Canon 9 of the Synod of Auxerre held in 578 AD and the synodal statutes of St Boniface prohibited women singing in church.[12] The Reform Synod of Paris held in 829 AD recorded the following:

> In some provinces it happens that women press around the altar, touch the holy vessels, hand the clerics the priestly vestments, indeed even dispense the body and blood of the Lord to the people. This is shameful and must not take place . . . No doubt such customs have arisen because of the carelessness and negligence of the bishops.[13]

The second Pseudo-Isidorian Letter which was ascribed to Pope Soter of the second century but which later proved to be a forgery dating from the middle of the ninth century records:

> It has been reported to the Holy See that consecrated women and nuns among you have been touching the holy vessels and the sacred linen. No one who knows what is right will doubt that this deserves disapproval and blame. Hence we declare on the ground of authority of the Holy See that you put a stop to all this as soon as possible, and prevent this plague from spreading over the provinces.[14]

The world has changed and all those prohibitions now seem so ridiculous. However, we should not feel too smug. The shocking discrimination against women serving on the altar continued in our twentieth century Church in Canon 813 (ii) of the Code of Canon Law until it was repealed by the new Code in 1983.

789, Admonitio 4 and 17, Hanover, 1883, 54–55.

12. Synod of Auxerre, Charles Joseph Héfélé, *Histoire des Conciles d'après les documents originaux*, translated by Abbé Delarc, tome 3 (Paris: Adrien le Clere et Co, 1870), 583; Statuta Quaedam Sancti Bonifacii, Joannes Dom Mansi, *Sacrorum Conciliorum nova et amplissima Collectio*, tome XII, col 385, Canon XXI,Antonius Zatta, Florence, 1766, Cf Migne, PL vol 89 col 822, Canon XXI.
13. Concilium Parisianse VI, Joannes Dom Mansi, *Sacrorum Conciliorum nova et amplissima Collectio*, tome XIV, Antonius Zatta, Venice, 1769, col 565; Charles Joseph Héfélé, *Histoire des Conciles,d'après les documents originaux*, translated by Dom Leclercq, tome IV, pars 1 (Paris: Letougey et Ané, 1911), 67; Monumenta Germaniae Historica, Legum Sectio III, Tome II Pars II, Concilia Aevi Karolini, 639–640.
14. *Isidori Mercatoris Collectio Decretalium*, Epistola Sotheris Papae, PL vol 130 col 119.

i. A priest may not celebrate Mass without a minister who will attend him and make replies.

ii. The minister serving Mass should not be a woman unless, in the absence of a man, and for just cause, she abides by the rule that she makes her replies from the body of the church ('ex longinquo') and agrees not to approach the altar.

Congar recorded in his Council Journal that in March 1963 Cardinal Léger of Canada had told him that he had been speaking to the new French ambassador to the Quirinal (Armand Bérard) and that the Pope, good Pope John XXIII, had confided to him—'I want to shake off the imperial dust that has accumulated on the throne of St Peter since the time of Constantine'. Good for him!

In 1975, a well-known French journalist and novelist, Jacques Duquesne, published a conversation he had had with a French Dominican who was an historian and theologian, for years in charge of the study programme for his Order at the Saulchoir—Père Marie-Dominique Chenu. In the course of the conversation, Chenu spoke of the Church's *memoire subversive*, her subversive memory.

> Remembering the past, returning to the sources is always a revolutionary experience, because it is a return to the source of creative energy. And this power always puts into question all the superstructures which have accumulated in the course of time. Not that the superstructures are without value, but it is always necessary to relativise them. A return to the original intuitions transforms the image we have of the machinery.[15]

In the modern era, our Church and all the others are faced with the fruits of the enlightenment, with the awesome discoveries of science, with a multitude of functioning, often hostile philosophies, with the rise of atheism, the education of the masses and vast possibilities provided by intergalactic means of communication. The old ways and the tired formulas of 'truth' no longer cut the mustard. The people have turned off. The infallible pope, the distant bishops and the clergy have frittered away or spoiled any credibility they once enjoyed. The simple, life-giving message of Jesus is now found in a poisoned waterhole. What's to be done?

---

15. *Jacques Duquesne interroge le Père Chenu*, 'les interviews', Le Centurion, 1975, Paris, 62.

In dialogue with the world and talking among ourselves

In our modern, scientifically dominated and diverse world, there are two areas of challenge facing Christianity and our Church. The first is on the level of ideas, and the second, on the level of the institution and its organisation—the first involves a dialogue with the world, the second demands an honest talk among ourselves.

On the level of ideas, some of the basic challenges for our Church down the track are:

i. To discover fresh, contemporary ways of thinking and talking about the divinity.
ii. To wrestle with the all-pervasive problem of Evil in all its forms, and to find new ways of integrating the terrifying experience of death, cruelty, suffering, war, bigotry into our view of the world, of salvation and of a loving God.
iii. To re-think the significance of the person of Jesus, and to find relevant ways of talking about him.
iv. To find new ways of thinking and talking about our Church.
v. To find a way of fostering a healthy attitude to the human body, to sexuality and to material creation.
vi. To find a way of embracing the discoveries of the secular sciences, of understanding the force as well as the limitations of the scientific method, and of harmonising our faith life and its fundamental tenets with the amazing and expanding world of science.

On the level of the institution, some of the areas in which we need to conduct an honest conversation among ourselves are:

i. The selection, training and appointment of Church leaders—popes, bishops, cardinals, priests and other ministers.
ii. The suppression of all forms of privilege and clericalism.
iii. The identification and encouragement of new ministries.
iv. To find the freedom Jesus and his Gospel promised, while remaining faithful to his message and obedient to the Spirit of the New Covenant.
v. To return to the evangelical demands of simplicity and to witness to Christ's love for the poor and the under-privileged.

In dialogue with the world

A contemporary image of God.
'What is divinity if it can come only in silent shadows and in dreams?'
   (*Sunday Morning* by Wallace Stevens).

A good question.

This is THE question to be asked and answered, inevitably only in silent shadows and dreams, by contemporary men and women of faith—of any faith. My instinct, however, is that when the name of God is mentioned, or when the word 'God' creeps into a normal conversation, the speaker, whether a Catholic, a Protestant, a Moslem a pagan or a non-believer, has little or no knowledge, or perhaps only an infantile image of who that particular being might be.

The way communities have had of talking and thinking about their particular deity or deities has varied throughout the centuries and from culture to culture. The way our Church and Christians at large have spoken about their God, and the way they have addressed him (inevitably 'him') in prayer, is also a sobering story of radical change. In broad strokes, I want to showcase the rainbow of colours men and women have used to paint a picture of the God in whom they have put their faith and whom they have worshipped, and I would like to trace briefly how the field has evolved. I am well aware that each stage in the evolutionary process is a complicated study in itself, and I don't want to present myself as having more than a superficial knowledge of the subject, especially since it is almost forty years since I have done any serious academic work in theology.

We have only to reflect for a moment how the ancient Greeks and Romans portrayed their gods and goddesses, and the whole spirit-world in their myths and epic literature. A complicated, ever-changing world. A community of gods, with their own laws and hierarchical structure, had gathered on Mount Olympus. At the top were twelve great gods and goddesses, with Jupiter in sovereign charge. Below these first-grade players was a team of seconds, and below them, a group of divine courtiers and hangers-on—muses, graces, nymphs. We read of the exploits and the changing moods of Jupiter (or Jove or Zeus) and his wife, the queen of the gods, Juno (or Hera). Mars (or Ares) was the god of war. Venus (or Aphrodite) the goddess of love and beauty. Neptune ruled the oceans and Pluto, the realms of the dead. Bacchus (or Dionysus) was the god of wine and riotous, unbridled fun; Momus, the god of laughter; Iris the goddess of the rainbow and Minerva (or Athena) the goddess of wisdom. The Satyrs were deities in control of woods and fields. From what we read, these divine beings were promiscuous, unpredictable, extremely fickle and ruled by jealousy, ambition and a range of diagnosable, psychotic conditions—just like us, but all very foreign to us Christians.

The ancestors of the Jewish people, before Moses and Abraham, worshipped many gods and offered human sacrifices to appease them, but gradually they became known in the region as the people who gave their allegiance to one God only, whose name could not be sounded or written.

In their sacred literature, the Jewish people spoke of their God as the creator of the heavens and the earth, and provider of all good things. He was masculine, of course—powerful, wise, demanding, punishing and forgiving—a patriarchal figure par excellence. He came in many guises. He was presented as a shepherd, a friend of Job, a father, a lover, an ecstatic dancer, but also as a cruel destroyer, a punishing judge, the Lord of Hosts and a conquering warrior.

> Yahweh your God is in your midst,
> a victorious warrior.
> He will exult with joy over you,
> he will renew you by his love;
> he will dance with shouts of joy for you
> as on a day of festival.[16]

On occasions the Jewish God was vindictive, unreasonable and punitive. He could treat his own people harshly, and his people's enemies unjustly. His presence among his people was associated with the Ark of the Covenant in the desert and in the Temple's Holy of Holies. He had made himself manifest to Moses, his servant, in a bush burning on sacred ground, but Moses had not seen him. He had hid his face because he was afraid to look at God (Ex 2). He came to his chosen ones, his heroes and prophets, in dreams and visions. God's presence among his people was associated with thunder and

---

16. Zeph 3:17.

lightning, earthquakes, mountain tops, clouds and belching smoke (Ex 19). He was present to different ancient figures under different guises. See how he appeared to Jacob in a dream—

> And he dreamed that there was a ladder set up on the earth, and the top of it reached to heaven; and behold, the angels of God were ascending and descending on it! And behold the Lord stood beside him and said, 'I am the Lord, the God of Abraham your father and the God of Isaac . . . Behold, I am with you and will keep you wherever you go, and will bring you back to this land; for I will not leave you until I have done that of which I have spoken to you.' Then Jacob woke from his sleep and said, 'Surely the Lord is in this place; and I did not know it.'[17]

Witness how God appeared to the leader of his people in the desert. Moses used to take the tent of meeting and pitch it outside the camp, far away. Anyone who wanted to seek God used to leave the camp and go out to the tent of meeting. The people used to follow Moses out and watch him from the door of the tent. When he entered the tent, the pillar of cloud used to descend and stand guard at the door of the tent. The Lord used to speak to Moses face to face, 'as a man speaks to his friend' (Ex 33:11).

Since Moses was Yahweh's special friend, known to him by name, Moses asked God to show him his glory, but the Lord replied—

> 'I will make all my goodness pass before you, and will proclaim before you my name "The Lord"; and I will be gracious to whom I will be gracious, and will show mercy on whom I will show mercy. But you cannot see my face; for man shall not see me and live.' And the Lord said, 'Behold, there is a place by me where you shall stand upon the rock; and while my glory passes by I will put you in a cleft of the rock, and I will cover you with my hand until I have passed by; then I will take away my hand, and you shall see my back; but my face shall not be seen.'[18]

In the First Book of Samuel, chapter 3, the Jewish community recorded that God appeared to the boy Samuel in the evening time, just before

---

17. Gen 28:12-13, 15-17.
18. Ex 33:19-23.

sleep, while he was lying in the temple of the Lord where the ark of God was. The Lord spoke to him, but Samuel did not understand. He thought that Eli the prophet was calling out to him from somewhere nearby, but it was the Lord, and eventually Samuel understood. Samuel did not see God, but he was present and the young boy heard him.

And the Lord came and stood by, calling as at other times, 'Samuel! Samuel!'

Witness again how God appeared to the prophet Elijah in the cave, but only after a long and tiring journey to Sinai, the mount of God.

> 'And there he came to a cave, and lodged there for the night; and behold, the word of the Lord came to him, and he said to him, "What are you doing here, Elijah?". . . "Go forth and stand upon the mount before the Lord". And behold, the Lord passed by, and a great and strong wind rent the mountains, and broke in pieces the rocks before the Lord, but the Lord was not in the wind; and after the wind an earthquake, but the Lord was not in the earthquake; and after the earthquake a fire, but the Lord was not in the fire; and after the fire a still small voice. And when Elijah heard it, he wrapped his face in his mantle and went out and stood at the entrance of the cave. And behold, there came a voice to him and said . . .'[19]

God's presence was like the murmur, the whisper of a soft breeze, symbolising the spiritual dimension of the Lord and the intimacy of his encounter with his prophet.

The Jews also believed that their Yahweh listened to, and answered the prayers of his people, that he punished misdeeds and rewarded virtue, that he could be appeased by the sacrifice of animals and birds. He was the Holy One. These people believed that their God was with them, constantly by their side, shepherding, protecting, leading, but that he was unfathomable, mysterious, out of reach, awesome, beyond reason and understanding.

The image of God which Jesus invited his followers to embrace was the image of his Father, a prodigal father whose ways were not

---

19. I Kg 19:9-13.

our ways, who gave generously to undeserving servants, who waived debts and forgave sinners, who could be encountered in deserts and on high mountains. This was the face of God which was revealed in the early Christian literature, especially in the Gospels. God numbered the hairs of our head, dressed the flowers and fed the birds of the field—someone involved, caring and careful—but mysterious. In order to be perfect as our heavenly Father is perfect, in order to be sons and daughters of our Father in heaven, a Christian must follow the example of this God and love his enemies and pray for those who persecute her, because the God of the Christians makes the sun rise on the wicked and the good, and sends rain on the just and the unjust (Mt 5:44–45).

In the Jewish community as well as in the early Christian Church, a disturbing, ambiguous and confusing message about God challenged the man of faith. The believer was led to believe that God presented himself as the God of a covenant especially sealed between himself and his people. This solemn contract involved allegiance and obedience on the part of his people, and in return, an exclusive love and fidelity guaranteed by God. Yet, despite this exclusive relationship, God remained the God of Everyman. He loves and protects everyone without distinction. While there was a host of Jewish people seeking his healing touch, Yahweh cured the pagan warrior, Naanan, of his leprosy (II Kg 5:1–14); and while his own people suffered terrible hunger during years of drought and famine, he chose to provide for the widow of Sarepta (I Kg 17:1–16). Jesus referred approvingly to both these events (Lc 4:27ff) and let his followers know that his mission, his God-given powers were not imprisoned in his community. His group of disciples did not have exclusive control over what was done in his name. God was not boxed in, but he could, and did work through non-commissioned officers who had no clear links to his community (Lc 9:49ff and Mt 9:38).

The God who emerges from our sacred text is present in the community, but never encountered face-to-face. He reveals himself as a being which is mysterious, ungraspable, uncontrollable and unpredictable. The believer is challenged to process dissonant information, to puzzle over paradoxes, to search for meaning in apparent contradictions, to discover a narrow path through the human undergrowth and to be content with sighs and whispers. She is lost for us in a cloud of unknowing. We can but glimpse, as in a mirror darkly, not face-to-face, some dim traces, some indistinct footprints in the sand, rumours like a soft breeze only suggesting where she has passed. He reveals himself, even in the sacred literature, like fossils hidden in sandstone. Her ways are not our ways; his thoughts are not our thoughts.

Now let's jump into the ocean of another era. The Christian notion of God took on new tints and contours as the community grew, as the Church became subject to new influences and became embedded in new cultures. Under the sway of Plato and neo-Platonism, of Aristotle and the various schools of theology in the Middle Ages, the personality of this supreme being was set out in clear propositions and defended by allegedly rational argument. He (always He) was omnipotent, omniscient, omnipresent, and eternal. God's existence as well as his personality traits could be proved rationally. This was more the God of the philosophers and by embracing this mindset, the Church lost a large element of the mysterious and ambiguous dimension of the divine.

Let us jump again. When I was growing up in Neutral Bay in the 1940's and 1950's, we visualised heaven as 'up there' and full of angels, Hell 'down there' and full of smoke, and God as an old man with a long white beard, on a throne, surrounded by choirs of angels and saints on clouds. He kept a written record of good deeds and evil, and as the judge of everyman, would condemn his own creatures to Hell for trivial offences, and for all eternity. He would purify those he loved in an oppressive gaol of purgation. He heard and answered prayers, especially if our faith was strong enough to move mountains.

While I was thinking about what I wanted to say about the divinity, I was having lunch with one of my ex-priest friends who also was ordained over fifty years ago, married with children and, like myself, a regular at Sunday Mass. I asked him whether he had any problem reconciling the idea of 'our Father in heaven' who listened to our prayers, who counts the hairs of our head and feeds the birds of the air with the slaughter of innocent children in Newtown Connecticut, with famine in Africa, thousands of refugees wandering the earth, disease, earthquakes and other natural disasters. He thought for a moment and reducing my enquiry to a very personal level, said that he had a deep faith in Providence. Many things had happened in his life which could only be explained by the intervention of Providence, and by way of example, he said that when he had been a priest and in charge of a large parish, he was having trouble answering the telephone and the door while the priests were at table. The intrusions were proving inconvenient for the household, so he had employed a senior lady to attend the door and the telephone during the evening meal. The problem was that she couldn't speak English well and misunderstood simple instructions. She had begun to realise she was in trouble and that her new job was in jeopardy, so she recommended that my priest friend employ her daughter to do her work while she moved on to something else. He had met the daughter, fallen in love and eventually married. As far as he was concerned, the whole happy story was Providence at work. God had been looking after him. I was a little startled to listen to his uncomplicated worldview. In some ways it's unfortunate and disturbing, but my faith is more tortured and torturous. For me, looking for the caring hand of Providence at work in the modern world is not a comfortable journey.

In *the Pastoral Constitution on the Church in the Modern World*, the bishops addressed a message of hope and compassion to 'the world of humanity' (para 2) and focused the Church's 'attention on the world of man, the whole human family along with the sum of those realities in the midst of which that family lives' (para 2). The bishops shone a light on atheism as the most serious problem of the contemporary world.

> For it is the function of the Church, led by the Holy Spirit who renews and purifies her ceaselessly, to make God the Father and His Incarnate Son present and in a sense visible (para 21).

Now, when in modern times an infantile image of God has proven so superficial and unsatisfactory, and the brazen assertions of atheistic commentators so infallibly stated, a believer is challenged to discover new images, richer metaphors to mediate a genuinely contemporary experience of the divine, of transcendence, of the refined focus of awe and reverence. This is a profound challenge, and I am not about to meet and answer it in this essay. Tampering with any man or woman's understanding of God can have catastrophic repercussions in their life. This has to be a delicate and slow process, but one on which each of us has to embark, hopefully with the help of our Christian community and our Church, if we are going to live comfortably and function effectively in the modern world.

A Christian believes that our Father God, his Word and their Spirit are at the core of everything which exists, here on earth as well as in the distant galaxies, large or small—every animal, each individual who exists or has ever existed. Divine life is part of the web and weave of my being, of our being. God is not male or female. He or She is not human, though we are so finite that we can only conceive of this faceless being as like ourselves, dressed in our clothes, under our guise. She is not constricted by the laws which govern us and our universe, which control our minds or our systems of law. The search for God is a confusing and mysterious fumbling.

I don't want you to think I have any idea what God looks like, or what it means to call him the Almighty, or her All Powerful, Eternal and ever-living. These epithets sound good and they serve to put this divine being outside and beyond my tiny world of experience. Of course, I do not know what God is like, but I believe in Jesus and in life, in the world, in creation, and I trust that this mysterious being knows me through and through. I reflect on what a child knows and feels as he is developing in the womb of his mother, how limited his world is, how unreflective and primitive in contrast to what his mother knows and feels as he is wrapped in her flesh, and what it is like for this creature to discover the experience of love and trust, to learn to dance and sing, to talk and to know the warmth of his mother, to fix his eyes on her and to recognise her face, to be at-one and to know that he and his mother are one. I was mesmerised by the sight of my grand-son, Charlie, as a baby—happy, relaxed in his mother's arms, staring into her eyes, fully present to her, trusting her, totally absorbed by her, but as yet unable to describe her or name her. She knew him and thrilled at his existence, but he did not know her as his mother, as an individual person although he could recognise her voice, respond to her call, feel at home in her embrace and register when she was absent. I cannot say much more. Jesus was a member of my tribe who was close to God and he has taught me almost all I know of value. Like Charlie, like the enwombed baby, I see now as in a cloud, in a dream, amid shadows, vaguely, and that has to be enough.

From my own personal experience, I have found that a man of faith is better enlightened by the lives and revelations of the mystics —St Paul, St John, Dionysius the Pseudo-Aeropagite, John of the

Cross, Teresa of Avila, Eckhart, Hildegard—than by the schoolmen of the Middle Ages, the neo-Scholastics of the nineteenth century or any College of Cardinals. In their cells, in the desert or on mountain tops, the mystics explore the corners of the galaxy in search of God's presence. Simple catechetical answers and neat, frozen formulas no longer answer the call of the human heart. I have found spiritual nourishment in Francis of Assisi, the poems of St John of the Cross, the Elegies of Rainer Maria Rilke and his Sonnets of Orpheus, in the Poems of TS Eliot and Gerard Manly Hopkins, in the novels of Patrick White, of David Malouf and especially the *grand oeuvre* of Marcel Proust, the cartoons of Michael Leunig and the overpowering and transcendent music of Beethoven and Bach, Wagner or Mahler.

In his journal entry of Tuesday 30 March, 1965, Congar encourages this search—

> Our epoch is at last overcoming the divorce introduced between mysticism and theology; the study of the Fathers has been both a cause and a result of this.[20]

The problem of evil

Evil in the modern world is confronting for Everyman, but she is especially troubling for those who believe in a personal God. Horrible murders. Unbearable suffering. Earthquakes. Bushfires. Bashings. Rapes. Tsunamis. Torture. Shocking, gratuitous cruelty to animals. Sexual abuse of children. And to top it off, Death.

We can't escape the terrible forces of Evil in all her guises. None of us, however strong or rich. With the modern media, wicked men and evil deeds, cosmic catastrophes and family tragedies are in our face daily, and we cannot help but ask—Why? That agonising, cosmic question—WHY?

Help me to understand. Or maybe just to accept stoically, heroically. We pray to relieve pain or hardship, but our heavenly Father does not intervene. Some of us believe that he could if he wished, if he knew, do something to protect us, to preserve us, to change the course of the world, of history. And he doesn't. Why? Why didn't he create a perfect world? Why not create perfect men and women? So much

---

20. Yves Congar, *My Journal of the Council*, 747.

senseless suffering. Are sin and guilt somehow woven into the web and weave of his creation? Are suffering, loss, trauma, death essential components of the human condition? Is evil a hydra-headed monster which will eventually devour us all?

> Q. Who is God?
>
> A. God is the Creator of heaven and earth, and of all things and the Supreme Lord of all.
>
> Q. Can God do all things?
>
> A. God can do all things.[21]

Some Christians believe that God can, and sometimes does even now, intervene here and there, in some special, exclusive and dramatic way, in the affairs of man. Miracles do happen, even in our faithless world. They believe that God, or his Son's mother, or some local saint, or perhaps an apprentice saint, pierces the mysterious veil or the cold, hard steel shield between heaven and earth, and touches this one, but not those thousands over there, cures that one, but leaves millions in pain. But if he can do this for one, why not for the many? Is God truly the father of everyone? Does he care? Does he love each of us without exception? Speak to me. Help me to explore this agonising puzzle. My inherited idea of God must be wrong.

When one fateful evening the then Cardinal Archbishop of Sydney, Cardinal Pell, was challenged on a national Australian television program, *Q&A*, to address the problem of Evil, from my point of view he failed us miserably. Our heavy-weight Vatican representative, our eminent religious leader could only manage to observe that evil was indeed a fearful problem and that when he arrives in heaven, this will be the very first question he will discuss with God. Well, bully for him. In the meantime, he'll let that ball go through to the keeper, without even an attempt to play at it.

Not good enough. We don't expect him, or anyone, to have THE answer, but a few words to help us deal in some way with this overshadowing daily torment would be a help. No one has THE answer, but this universal problem has to be addressed by our Church leaders. They cannot vacate the field and leave it to the God deniers

---

21. *The Thrupenny Catechism*, fifth edition, 1945, questions 1 and 13, 11-12.

to mock. I note in passing that two Australian Jesuits have recently published their reflections of the problem of Evil—Richard Leonard, *Where the Hell is God?*[22] (Mahwah, NJ: Paulist Press, 2010), and John Cowburn, *The Problems of Suffering and Evil*[23] (Milwaukee: Marquette University Press, 2012).

Thinkers, philosophers, theologians and preachers down the ages have wrestled with this problem of evil. Some have thought that the only solution was to be found in positing an ugly god of Evil, a fearsome demiurge, a type of all-powerful devil working energetically with his wrecking ball on the creation of the sublime God of all goodness. The Jewish people re-told the myth of a fall from grace of Adam, tempted by Eve. St Augustine took up this story and developed a theory of original sin passed on by copulation, and the power of his insights seemed to satisfy the West, at least until the penetrating questioning of the modern era. His answers were simply repeated in the little Green Catechism for us to learn by heart.

> Q. What is original sin?
>
> A. Original sin is the sin which is inherited from our First Parents, and in which we were born.
>
> Q. Who were our First Parents?
>
> A. Our First Parents were Adam and Eve, the first man and woman.
>
> Q. Who tempted our First Parents to eat the forbidden fruit?
>
> A. The devil tempted them to eat the forbidden fruit.
>
> Q. Who is the devil?
>
> A. The devil is one of the fallen angels whom God cast out of Heaven.

---

22. (New York: Paulist Press, 2010).
23. (Milwaikee: Marquette University Press, 2012).

Some would have us accept that Evil is at least partially explained by the fact that the creator chose to create his human handiwork to live in freedom, that man's deeds should be determined by his free will and that in the end God will judge the living and the dead.

The Church has to be able to say something, something meaningful, something over target on this awful topic. Sin and culpability are endemic to man. Suffering and death are at the centre of human existence and at the very heart of the Christian message. Our Christian existence is essentially, existentially tragic. The life of Jesus challenges us to meet evil face-to-face, to take it by the throat, to see it for what it is, in all its personifications and shapes, to name it, to throttle it, to overpower it and dispossess it. The cross of Jesus confronts evil in all its forms. The rejection of Jesus and his counter-cultural message, his betrayal and his violent death are interpreted by Christians as a living proof their Father-God has entered into the death and darkness, the pain and cruelty, the irrationality of our world.

At the beginning of his ministry, in the wilderness, Jesus confronted Evil in person and was tempted, like Adam and Eve in the Genesis myth, to embrace a false set of values, to assume an arrogant and proud pose and challenge the divine. He was encouraged to work a miracle by changing stones into bread to relieve his hunger, and tempted to act stupidly in the expectation that God and his angels would step in to provide comfort. In confronting evil in all her forms, remember—'Man shall not live by bread alone', since there is a hidden, mysterious dimension to his existence; and 'You shall not put the Lord your God to the test', since we are, after all, only human specks in the cosmos.

Our early Church believed that Jesus won a decisive victory over all forms of evil. He triumphed over death and defeated Evil in all its forms —bullying, torturing, tormenting, assaulting, prejudice, exclusion, hatred, greed, persecution. His presence among his followers after his death (which is after all the mystery of the Resurrection) was the guarantee that Evil had been defeated, and while Evil is still with us, in our midst, hurting us and all mankind, we live in the certain hope that ultimately Good, our God will be seen to have prevailed in the crushing victory of his Son.

The Church does have something intelligent and meaningful to say about sin and culpability, about suffering and death, about the human condition. No magical solutions. No permanent fix, at least this side of the grave—but something to say that makes some enigmatic sense, like the poet Rainer Maria Rilke addressing the nauseous subject of abortion.

> Look, I've been calling a lover. But she wouldn't come
> alone . . . Other girls could rise out
> of those crumbling graves and stand . . .
> Life is glorious here. You girls know it, even you
> who seem to have gone without it—you who sank under
> in the cities' vilest streets festering like open sewers.
> For there was one hour for each of you, maybe
> less than an hour, some span between two whiles
> that can hardly be measured, when you possessed Being.
> All. Your veins swelled with existence.
> *The Seventh Elegy.*

The meaning of Jesus to the modern world

For over a hundred years now, Christian and secular scholars, with the sophisticated tools of historical research and hermeneutical techniques, have been engaged in an intense study of the foundational literature of Christianity—the Gospels, the letters of Paul, the story of the development of the early Church. Many of our simplistic assumptions about Jesus and his followers have come under question. Some of our cherished beliefs have been undermined. The time has come once more to re-think the significance of the person of Jesus for our modern world. What can his life, lived so long ago in a remote region of the Roman Empire, mean to us? Should it mean anything? How can we re-interpret his message so that its freshness and its force take root in the heart of modern man? What does it mean, if anything, to say that Jesus is Lord, or Messiah, or Saviour, Son of God, Lamb of God? Does the image of the Sacred Heart of Jesus speak to the contemporary world as we would wish? Or rather, does it confuse, alienate, amuse and distract? Does the ancient, Anselmian explanation of God's plan for salvation, based on the notion of sin and satisfaction, of debt and repayment, find echoes in our modern society? Or must we find another way to interpret Jesus' special mission?

There is an untapped tradition running from the Pauline epistles and the Joannine literature, through St Irenaeus' writings in the second century to Teilhard de Chardin in the twentieth—a tradition traced by Matthew Fox and developed by our own Paul Collins and others—a tradition which bypasses the now unpalatable ideas of a petty, offended Godhead who is appeased in some way by the blood sacrifice of his only Son. Our Church could speak more convincingly to the modern world about Jesus by embracing the evolutionary vision of Jesus as the recapitulation of all things in heaven and on earth, as the Alpha and Omega of God's salvific plan, as the fulfillment of the Father's plan to divinise mankind and his whole creation in the person of Jesus.

What's the particular dimension of Jesus's life which might appeal to a man or woman touched with the spirit of the modern, secular world? Perhaps a contemporary religious person should reflect on Jesus's role as a revealer of the awesome, transcendent, mysterious dimension of all reality, the image or reflection of what God is like, how God relates to mankind and to the world—with intimacy, informally, lovingly, carefully, with compassion and forgiveness, generously. His life lived and described for us in the Gospels is an image, given to us, as to how God lives with us in the world—close to the earth, feet on the ground, toes in the mud—as to how God wants us to be present to him—like Jesus, prayerfully, quietly, confidently, trustfully, in the middle of crowds, in little groups of friends, at parties, respectfully, alone in the desert, reflectively on mountain-tops, full of awe and reverence, and simple faith. In this historical person walking the fields and alleyways of Palestine, God is joined to earth, and earth to heaven. He was, and remains God's teacher in the world, God's intimate companion, his Prophet, his messenger, his revelation—and God's challenge to mankind as to how to live life forever in God's presence.

In this day and age, our Christian community is longing for leaders, for teachers with courage and imagination who can speak to the modern world. The old formulas have served their purpose, but they are wrinkled and tired. They have been done to death. It is obvious that they no longer carry the message to the world.

New images, new metaphors, fresh theological visions which can find echoes in the culture of today and speak to men and women in the world. Christians were not commissioned by Jesus to talk interminably to themselves, repeating the same old formulas, singing the same hymns, performing the same old rituals. We are called to carry on what was handed on to us by Jesus and to preach the good news to strangers, to pagans and to the poor. We stand in need of poets, writers, theologians, prophets, visionaries to accompany us on our journey of discovery. Let the flowers blume.

This is an immense challenge confronting all Christians, so let me give you an example of what I think is possible.

Some years ago, as Archbishop of Melbourne, the now Cardinal George Pell attempted, unsuccessfully, to remove a scandalous piece of sculpture from a Melbourne art exhibition. He formed the opinion that the particular artifact was blasphemous and sacrilegious—and perhaps it was. In some people's eyes, it certainly was. On behalf of the city and his Archdiocese, he had sought a court order to have the sculpture removed from the public domain. Of course, his stand generated controversy in the Australian press and among outraged artists. George could stir up a storm. He loved to cause trouble. The forces of liberty, of free speech and artistic expression rose up to challenge the medieval shackles of religion. The Archbishop summoned all followers of Christ to demonstrate their respect for the sacred. We were told that our Christian faith demanded expressions of outrage in the face of the public insult.

The shunned South American artist had exhibited a tortured figure of Christ on a cross, encased in a glass container which was full of yellow urine. Whose? We were never told. Presumably, hopefully, the artist's own. No one alleged that his work was not authentic.

Sacrilege?—Perhaps. Blasphemy?—Maybe. A sacred object of profound, religious significance had been desecrated. Many members of the community were seriously offended, and they all assumed that God was extremely displeased.

The urine might have been simply a pathetic fetish of a crazy artist. Maybe Andres Serrano's personal cross was that he suffered from a paraphiliac condition, achieving his sexual gratification by arousing stimulating fantasies at the thought, the smell, the taste of urine. Or maybe 'Piss Christ' was a distasteful joke, or an angry, alienated artist's frustrated shout at the verities of our society.

Inspired by the obsessions of people like the Marquis de Sade, modern surrealist artists were at the time engaged in a revolution of obscenity in our western world. By exploring the dark recesses of the mind, feeling a forbidden path through the inscrutable secrets of desire, Salvador Dali and others like him had stirred a revolt inside the mind and heart rather than in the streets of Paris. They pedalled revolting images of death, of Time wasted and exhausted, of human waste as excrement. By collecting disgusting fragments of reality, searching the archives of debauchery, as rag pickers and scavengers, the surrealists provided impetus to our age's self-destruction. Suicides were becoming fashionable. Self-destruction became the hallmark of modernism and the only credible reaction to an absurd world. Some artists and businessmen sought to transform the world into a global brothel, a cesspool of human experience, a garbage bin for men to rummage in.

The intense sexual experience which has kept mankind fascinated over the centuries and a continuing presence on the globe has been deconstructed, re-contextualised, reinterpreted, trivialised, commercialised, and reduced to the status of entertainment. Sex was no longer mainly a participatory sport. To enhance the interests of big business, our modern society was being titillated, entertained, distracted, pre-occupied with watching complete strangers wrestle, cavort, twist, entwine, grind, distort their bodies on screen, while the viewers' own intimate relations were wrinkling, drying up and corrupting.

The sexual revolution of our age has proved to be a powerful act of anarchy against our social taboos, against Christian values and principles, and especially against the Roman Catholic Church whose unfortunate obsession with sex has been so public, so negative, so detailed, so Manichean. The sexual and artistic revolution of the 60's has been taken over and exploited by big business, by international corporations and the entertainment industry.

Now men and women undress in public, on the screen, and perform intimate, sacred, secret acts under the gaze of onlookers. They perform for us on television. Raw pornography is available in shops or, for the discreet, through Her Majesty's mail. Sex is no longer a means to continue the clan, or to express intimacy, love, commitment, fidelity, to strengthen family bonds, or even to entertain a friend—it is far too serious and commercial for laughter. It's become a commodity like MacDonalds. It's a form of mass entertainment, a potent method of increasing sales and profits. The artist, Andres Serrano, might have been caught up in this dirty modern movement.

And 'Piss Christ' might have been more than an expression of some unhealthy fetish, or a crass act of revolt against accepted values, against the churches and religious experience. It might have been a 'work of art' which reflected the mindset of Dali and the surrealists —confronting, offensive, destructive, sacrilegious, blasphemous and verging on a despair which leads inevitably to suicide—in short, a genuine expression of the world of modernism. Either way, as a national religious leader, Cardinal Pell might have been justified in stepping out into the market-place and engaging the pagans on behalf of his people.

But there was a totally different interpretation available to the Archbishop. This 'work of art' was out there, in the public domain, on show, inviting public discussion. It no longer belonged to the artist. He had created the work and delivered it to the public for acceptance or rejection, for scrutiny, for us to search it and perhaps find some significance in it. His purpose in fashioning the object was in a sense, no longer germane.

According to Christian belief, the crucifixion itself was a sacrilege far more intense and horrific than any Serranto act of profanation. Yet for Christians with faith, this act was permeated with redemptive, liberating power. A sacred person, blessed by his father, a messenger of God, the Messiah, was arrested, stripped, spat on, whipped, mocked, crowned with bloody thorns, and crucified. The sweat, the cries of pain inflicted, the nails driven, the blood oozing, the torment by the soldiers and officials, the flow of blood and water from the corpse's side, screamed of the violation of someone precious to God. The players all contributed to an event, a sacrilegious event, a flesh event, which was for Christians, religious, sacred and mysterious.

The soldiers, the Jewish leaders, the bureaucrats, the Roman governor, all shared in what became for Christians down the ages a redemptive event. It was the blood and the wood, the jeers and the violent, profane death which were for them redemptive. Bodily fluids and excretions produced salvation.

Over the intervening centuries, these terrible earth events were removed from the mud of the ordinary, from the profane, and gradually etherealised, sanitised, abstracted, varnished, polished, standardised, twisted into a different shape and made to appear in their new clothes as though they were the reality.

From the beginning, the simple cross of broken wood became the sign of redemption, just as the pouring of water became the sign of life, or the breaking of ordinary bread, the sign of sharing in the death of the Lord. No vestments, no candles, no incense, no church building and no formulas.

Later, much later, a human figure was affixed to the bare cross, sometimes wearing the vestments of a bishop or an emperor, with a crown, not of thorns but of diamonds and sapphires, a figure resting comfortably, in triumph on the cross, in glory. Jesus might have been amazed to see himself portrayed in death as a Byzantine emperor, but all the time, the reality was the dirty, suffering, bleeding Jesus.

The Christian community down the ages has felt free to reinterpret the bare crucifixion event, to present it in new clothes, to cover the harsh, nude reality, to hide the earthiness of the pain, to re-mythologise the message and imagine that the person of the crucified Jesus gave credibility to the institutionalised form of the Gospel.

The same transfiguration of the figure of Jesus occurred as the Church gathered secular strength and drifted far from its roots in Palestine. At first Jesus had been proclaimed and preached, but never depicted under any human form. Later, a figure of a tender shepherd appeared in the candle-lit shadows of the Roman catacombs. In later, imperial times, he appeared in colourful mosaics as a Roman Emperor; then as a dark-haired, dark-eyed, severe, monastic figure in the icons of Byzantium and Russia; as the lord of the province in the age of feudalism; the elegant scholar and courtier in the Middle Ages; the psychologically perfect human being during the Renaissance; as the sad, saccharine, wounded Sacred Heart in the times of French piety and devotion.

The mundane, secular, creational, earthy reality which for believers had resonated with redemptive power was gradually elevated into some artificially sacred dimension, hidden, mystified, distorted, varnished, and integrated into a system in which the exercise of power could be controlled and mediated through an ever-tightening institution.

From another point of view, the ecclesiastical demeanour of a member of the College of Cardinals, with his vestments, his ethereal language, his elevated position (some might say, not indistinguishable from the religious leaders of Jesus' time), might be sacrilegious in that it amounts to a violation, a profanation of what Jesus really stood for.

The confronting image of 'Piss Christ' could have been a powerful reminder of the gutsiness of Jesus, the fleshiness of his significance, the redemptive and creational value of human waste such as sweat, blood, breathe, vomit and the by-products of death.

It is no longer easy to tell what is genuine and what fake, what is truly religious, what is humbug. In our pluralistic society, we are bombarded on every side with a cacophony of contradictory interpretations. Things and people are often not what they seem. In a monolithic community, an exclusively Christian society for example, only one politically correct interpretation of a set of facts was presented, perhaps even imposed. No voice could be heard above the figure of power, and no one would seek to utter a contrary view. Pope Benedict appeared to believe right to the end that we all live in this world of revealed certitude, of authorised trust—but he and his Curia mates reside in a fairyland.

On Monday 8 June 1964, Congar had a private audience with the pope. The discussion had ranged over a wide number of topics. The pope had praised a French layman, Jean Guitton, who he thought was able to make the Church's voice heard among the laypeople. 'I was cowardly. I did not dare tell him that that was only half true. I said nothing.'[24]

After the audience, Congar went to dine in the open air in the Piazza Navona with four of his Belgian confreres (Prignon, Philips, Moeller and Thils).

> We saw normal people again, to whom our byzantine intrigues would have absolutely NOTHING to say!'[25]

In our modern world, life is not so simple. Ecclesiastical authority, coupled to basic catechetical statements on law and order, virtue,

---

24. Yves Congar, *My Journal of the Council*, 558.
25. Yves Congar, *My Journal of the Council*, 557.

faith, blind acceptance, sin, sacrilege and obedience, does not neatly solve all questions. What appears as virtue may also be cowardice; what seems blasphemous, may be profoundly religious; what seems pontifically religious, may be pagan pomposity, or grubby politics, or an ugly, distorted emptying of something noble and precious.

The Archbishop did not give anyone a chance to reflect or to use this shocking artefact as a stimulus to a deeper religious understanding. A super-cleric dusted off his superman outfit and rushed out of the telephone box with all guns blazing, to crush the devil and his friends, and to defend what those in charge have defined as Orthodoxy. But he missed a golden opportunity to speak to the modern world and to present an original view of salvation and the Christian message which might have spoken to an alienated world. We should be forever looking for golden opportunities to reflect on the significance of Jesus. That's the challenge for us and our Church.

New ways of talking about the Church

While the history books might present her as an ordered, neat, disciplined institution, when you look beneath the surface and read between the lines, our Church, the Roman Catholic Church, has always been a bit of a rabble—fights, corruption, bribes for high offices, even for the highest, murders, arguments, sometimes vicious disputes, Mafia families mixed up with a few saints, a handful of scholars, an occasional energetic reformer and a mass of strugglers and dogsbodies. That's been our history, and just because in recent centuries we've experienced a tidal wave of pious devotions and a team of clerics intent on central control and an impeccable, powerful image, it does not alter the fact that we are still a bit of a rabble. That's our attraction—and the mystery of it. Jesus appears to us in rags and rubbish, hidden in the ordinary, under the appearances of bread and wine, just barely visible in flesh and blood. And to be one of his faithful followers, you have to be a bit of a stirrer, walking the narrow track not often trod, an outsider, a rebel like him. To be honest, it's always been a mess even at the best of times.

The modern world, full of the principles of liberty, equality and fraternity, challenges us as members to re-think and re-configure our image of the Church. Is it mainly an institution, or is it a sacred but inadequate sign of Christ's presence among us? Is it principally a loose conglomeration or federation of local communities of rough believers, or a global society, an international organisation with its headquarters in Rome and under the control of the pope and his Curia—or perhaps something in-between? What is the Church? And how can we introduce her, honestly, realistically, in all her glory and with all her flaws, to our brothers and sisters in the modern world?

The Church was originally a spontaneous community of believers who prayed together and shared what they had with each other—a tight-knit community which enjoyed some basic, structural leadership provided by a group of Apostles, and with Peter as their brother and leader. As the community expanded and the believers began to realise that the end of the world was not so imminent, tensions emerged, factions appeared, smudges, splotches, the sharing of possessions grew more difficult, and clearer, tighter structures began to be needed. Gradually, slowly, an institution emerged and began to take shape.

Since the revolutionary movements in Europe at the end of the eighteenth century, since the time of Pius IX and the First Vatican Council in the 1870s, especially since the development of instantaneous and global means of communications, as she was losing her temporal power and her political influence in the world, the institutional Church has tended gradually to become more and more alien in the world, more centralised in Rome, more defensive, threatened by the secular sciences and learning, more authoritarian, dogmatic and high-bound in inflexible laws. Our Church did not enthusiastically embrace the democratic processes, or industrialisation, or the swell and swirl of modern science and culture. The pope, like an absolute monarch, and his clerical bureaucrats isolated in Rome, have worked hard to resist change and to keep a close eye, a tight fist on every local church on the globe, even those as far away as Toowoomba.

In school and later in the seminary, I was taught that the one, holy, catholic and apostolic Church was a divinely founded, visible institution, with the pope at its head, with bishops obedient to him and in charge of local dioceses, priests in charge of parishes, religious nuns and brothers to teach, to run hospitals and pray, and lay men and women at the bottom of the pyramid whose duty it was to pray, obey, and pay. The Church of Rome was the one, true Church well-founded by Christ, and there was no salvation outside that organisation.

Known as the Mystical Body of Christ, she was a perfect society with her own system of government, her own capital, her own members and agents of power, her own language, feast days, system of laws and courts. Her own bank.

As the old Catechism said –

> Q. Where are true Christians to be found?
>
> A. True Christians are to be found in the true Church.
>
> Q. What do you mean by the true Church?
>
> A. The true Church is the society of all the bishops, priests and faithful under the one visible head appointed by Christ.
>
> Q. Which is the true Church?
>
> A. The true Church is the Holy Catholic Church.

When Pope John summoned the Council, the bishops from around the world came together to discuss their role in the modern world, to attempt to re-configure a more realistic, a more attractive image of the Church, to understand how they as bishops related among themselves and to the bishop of Rome, and how our Church could relate anew to the modern world. In their Dogmatic Constitution on the Church (*Lumen Gentium*), the bishops described the Church by using many different images and metaphors of biblical origin. In this way they invited Christians inside and outside the organisation to reflect on these rich metaphors in order to explore the mystery that is the Church. She was presented as the kingdom of Christ now present in mystery; a kind of sacrament or sign of intimate union with God, and of the unity of all mankind; the little flock of Christ (a pastoral image); the vineyard of God (an agricultural image); the temple of the Holy Spirit, the dwelling place and the house of God (a construction imagery); the spouse of the immaculate sacrificial Lamb (a matrimonial image); the mother of every Christian and of mankind; the Body of Christ who is, in turn, her head (a corporeal image); a community of faith, hope and charity; the visible assembly of Christ's followers; a society and a pilgrim people wandering in a foreign land; the new Israel; a fellowship of life, charity and truth. All wonderful metaphors to explore. But the image *par excellence* and the one which dominated the theological reflections of the Council fathers was 'the People of God'—a messianic people, a holy nation, a chosen race, a redeemed gathering which men and women become part of by faith and baptism, and which therefore included members of other Christian churches as well as those of our Roman Catholic Church.

According to this preferred metaphor, the Church sees herself as a grouping or gathering of many different and differing people who are on a journey together, at times wandering about in the desert, sometimes lost, or weary, or hungry, and at other times rejoicing and celebrating, sharing, dancing, interacting among themselves and with others, moving in and out of different cultures. This image allows, in fact demands that structures, powers and leadership roles develop, and change within the continuing life of the People, always subject to the emerging and changing needs and well-being of the tribe or mob. And the group, the People is the principal and dominant reality. Viewing the Church as a people, a tribe or a mob in which there is no line drawn between male or female, black or white, rich or poor, Jew or gentile, demands an accepting, inclusive, basically democratic mentality—no preferment, no privileges, no hierarchy of status.

This image of Church can be challenging to an institution, and disruptive to the life of an organisation. It can be a pretty crazy notion for the bachelors in the Curia because the metaphor, of its nature, implies a level of chaos, an element of swirl and turbulence, a degree of ebb and flow, or in other words, a dynamic life - and the structures, the ministries, the hierarchy, the law and regulations are there to facilitate and support the life and movement of the people, the mob, the crowd, not to overpower and corral them. The Church is not like a large bank, or an army trained, disciplined, ready for battle, or a club or lodge. It is more like a family, a tribe, a gathering of many, a movement.

We must learn to accept that we are the Church. The people of God —that's us. Without us, there is no point to the rules, the structures, the bishops or the pope. There is no Church without us. We give them meaning. They are our servants.

Creation, the human body and sexuality

> For thou lovest all things that exist,
> and hast loathing for none of the things which thou hast made,
> for thou wouldst not have made anything if thou hadst hated it.[26]

If the Church is to survive and thrive in the twentieth-first century, she faces an urgent call to develop a healthy attitude to the visible, material world, to the human body (which, to state the bleeding obvious, has been created by God), and to our human sexuality under all its forms. She must develop as quickly as possible a coherent theology of creation to support modern environmental concerns, animal welfare, to condemn all forms of cruelty towards, and torture of human beings and other animals, as well as to promote a positive, Christian outlook which will encourage all men and women to explore the sexual dimension and other aspects of their lives. Celibate males have dug the Church into a deep black pit and I suspect that living at the end of the yellow brick road in Rome, these men are generally unaware of how they are ignored by their own, and oblivious to the mockery they have generated for Jesus' community of believers.

Our Church's traditional and negative attitude to things material, to the earth, to animals other than the human species, to the body and to human sexuality is a heavy burden to carry in the modern world, and one which the celibate clergy certainly has not been able to lift. The Church, through the faithful, the pope and the bishops, individually and as a college, is a significant guardian of the Good News as revealed in the Bible and Tradition, but despite her claims, she is not the pre-eminent and authoritative interpreter of the dictates of the natural law which has been written in the hearts of every man and woman. Serious distortions occur when a powerful organisation claims too much power and authority for itself.

Throughout her life and for very complex reasons, our institution has indulged in a superfluity of talk about immaculate conceptions, virgin births, vows of virginity, compulsory promises of celibacy, too much concentration on copulation, on French letters and the pill, on bad thoughts, self-abuse and homosexual intercourse. And while

---

26. Wisdom 11:24.

the talk out of Rome has been angelic and supernatural, many of our religious leaders have not walked the walk, and of those that have gone the distance, many have paid a very heavy price. Not enough attention has been paid to the beauty and goodness of God's creation, to human intimacy, to a transforming flesh-love between a man and a woman, the exquisite beauty of the human body, to our God-given spontaneous drives and impulses and to the realities of human existence.

To understand why our Church is now so hung-up on questions of sexual orientation and behaviour, and on the question of women's role in the institution, we should tune in, at least once in our lifetime, to the twisted minds of Christian leaders like Quintus Septimius Florens Tertullian (ca 160-225), Gregory of Nazianzan (329-389), Augustine (354-430), John Chrysostom (ca 347-407), Thomas Aquinas (ca 1225-1274), Albert the Great (ca 1200-1280), as they talk disrespectfully about women, about bodies and sexual activity. We should try to fathom the world these men inhabited. Once you have read the authors, you will be in no doubt as to why our Church has persisted in imposing on us, by rules, by teachings, solemn declarations and condemnations, such an unholy misogynistic culture, such prurient attitudes which prevents her from saying anything meaningful to the modern world. Let us begin with Tertullian, Gregory Nazianzan and Augustine of Hippo.

> Do you not know that you are each an Eve? The sentence of God on this sex of yours lives in this age: the guilt must of necessity live too. You are the devil's gateway; you are the unsealer of that forbidden tree; you are the first deserter of the divine law; you are she who persuaded him whom the devil was not valiant enough to attack. You so carelessly destroyed man, God's image. On account of your desert, even the Son of God had to die.[27]

> Fierce are the dragons and cunning the asps, but women have the malice of both beasts.[28]

---

27. Tertullian, *De Cultu Feminarum Libri Duo*, bk 1, ch 1, PL vol 1 cols 1417–1419. Cf *On the Apparel of Women*, ch 1, Ante-Nicene Fathers, vol 4, edited by Alexander Roberts and James Donaldson (New York: Christian Literature Publishing Co,1885), 14.
28. Gregory of Nazianzan, *Poemata Moralia*, 32 vv 117–118, PG vol 37 col 925.

> What is the difference whether it is in a wife or a mother? It is still Eve the temptress that we must beware of in any woman . If it was good company and conversation that Adam needed, it would have been much better arranged to have two men together as friends, not a man and a woman.[29]

This popular theme of the pub mates, club comrades, lodges and football teams was taken up later, in the thirteenth century, by theologians and scholars such as Albert the Great and Thomas Aquinas. Both tried to persuade their students that women were good for procreation and that once that work was done, their usefulness was limited. For all other activities and for true companionship, a man is better served by another man. A woman can make no contribution to a man's intellectual life. For these intellectual giants, women were in truth developmentally retarded men. They do not fulfil nature's primary intention viz perfection. They are the weaker sex, with less physical and intellectual strength.[30] St Thomas believed that men have 'more perfect reason' than women,[31] and that because of a defect in their reasoning ability, like children and mentally ill persons, they are not permitted to act as witnesses in court proceedings.[32] But let us return to St Augustine and St John Chrysostom.

> I consider that nothing so casts down the manly mind from its heights as the fondling of women, and those bodily contacts which belong to the married state.[33]

> The whole of her bodily beauty is nothing less than phlegm, blood, bile, rheum, and the fluid of digested food. If you

---

29. St Augustine of Hippo, *De Genesi ad litteram*, Bk 9 ch 5, PL vol 34 col 396. Cf *The Literal Meaning of Genesis*, translated and annotated by John Hammond Taylor SJ, vol II (New York: Newman Press, 1982), 75.
30. Albert the Great, II sent 20, 1 and IV sent 26, 6. Thomas Aquinas, *Summa Theologiae*, I, q 52, a1 ad 2; q 92 a1.
31. *Summa Contra Gentiles*, III, 123.
32. *Summa Theologiae*, II. II q 70 a3.
33. St Augustine of Hippo, *Soliloquiorum Libri Duo*, bk 1, ch 10 PL vol 32 col 878 Cf Wolfgang Hormann, *Augustinus, Opera*, sect 1, pars IV, *Soliloquiorum libri duo*, de immortalitate animae, Corpus Scriptorum Ecclesiasticorum Latinorum Series, Vindobonai, Hoelder-Pichler-Tempsky, 1986. St Thomas Aquinas, *Summa Theologiae*, II. II, q151 De Castitate, art 3, ad 2, Marietti, Rome, 1952, 653.

> consider what is stored up behind those lovely eyes, the angle of the nose, the mouth and cheeks, you will agree that the well-proportioned body is merely a whitened sepulchre.[34]
>
> There are in the world a great many situations that weaken the conscientiousness of the soul. First and foremost of these are dealings with women. In his concern for the male sex, the superior may not forget the females, who need greater care precisely because of their ready inclination to sin. In this situation the evil enemy can find many ways to creep in secretly. For the eye of woman touches and disturbs our soul—and not only the eye of the unbridled woman, but that of the decent one as well.[35]

In reviewing the Church's attitude to the body, flesh, sex, marriage and creation, we should not bypass the Celtic traditions of the Penitentials which reflect the beliefs, the superstitions and practices of the Church in Ireland, in Britain and throughout Europe from about the sixth century to the tenth or eleventh century. The Penitential of Finnian of Clonard dates from the first half of the sixth century. Canon 46 advised and exhorted that married couples should regularly abstain from engaging in any sexual activity, and for lengthy periods.

> ... since marriage without continence is not lawful, but sin, and (marriage) is permitted by the authority of God not for lust but for the sake of children ... not for the lustful concupiscence of the flesh. Married people, then, must mutually abstain during three forty-day periods in each single year, by consent for a time, that they may be able to have time for prayer for the salvation of their souls; and on Sunday night or Saturday night they must mutually abstain, and after the wife has conceived he shall not have intercourse with her until she has borne her child ...[36]

---

34. St John Chrysostom, *Ad Theodoram lapsum*, para 14, PG vol 47 cols 297–299 Cf *An Exhortation to Theodore after his Fall*, The Nicene and Post-Nicene Fathers of the Christian Church, vol IX, *St Chrysostom*, edited by Philip Schaff DD, LL D, (Grand Rapids: Eerdmans Publishing Company), 103–104.
35. St John Chrysostom, *De Sacerdotio*, Bk 6 Chapter 8 PG vol 48 col 684. Cf The Nicene and Post-Nicene Fathers of the Christian Church, vol IX, 78–79.
36. John T McNeill and Helena M Gamer, *Medieval Handbooks of Penance*, a translation of the principal Libri Poenitentiales and selections from related documents (New York: Columbia University Press, 1938), 96.

The Penitential of abbot Cummean was in circulation in the Frankish Empire in the early ninth century and was probably known in Ireland in the seventh century. It provided the penances to be imposed for a whole variety of sins (the many forms of gluttony, avarice, anger, violence, pride, misuse of the sacred species etc), especially sins of a sexual nature—fornication by a bishop, a priest, a deacon, bestiality by clerics, sodomy, oral sex, kissing, defiling virgins, polluting glances, suggestive advances etc. Within this context, the Penitential provided—

> 30. He who is in a state of matrimony ought to be continent during the three forty-day periods and on Saturday and on Sunday, night and day, and in the two appointed week days, and after conception, and during the entire menstrual period.
>
> 31. After a birth he shall abstain, if it is a boy, for thirty-three (days); if a daughter, for sixty-six (days).

At the end of the twelfth century, Innocent III succeeded his uncle, Celestine III, as bishop of Rome. He was elected by the cardinals to be pope when he was thirty-six years old and only a cardinal deacon. As a deacon he showed his colours in an essay on 'The Misery of our Human Condition'.

> Oh the supreme ugliness of sexual pleasure! It not only makes the mind effeminate but the body sick; not only stains the soul but defiles the person as well . . . Sexual pleasure is preceded by lust and wantonness; it is accompanied by a foulsome stench and uncleanliness; it is followed by sadness and remorse. Man has been formed of dust, clay, ashes and, a thing far more vile, of the filthy sperm. Man has been conceived in the desire of the flesh, in the heat of sensual lust, in the foul stench of wantonness . . . Sexual intercourse is always infected—even in matrimony—with the desire of the flesh, with the heat of lust and with the foul stench of wantonness. Because of this, the union of the sexes itself is contaminated; whence, too, does the soul inherit the infection of sin . . . for in sexual intercourse one loses dominion over one's reason and thus sows ignorance; the heat of lust is enkindled and so anger is propagate; pleasure is satiated and concupiscence is contracted.

When we purchase a horse, an ass, a cow, a dress, a bed, a chalice or only a water-pot it is only after having first tried them out. But man's fiancé is scarcely shown him lest he reject her before marriage. After marriage, however, he must keep her in any case—be she ugly, stinking, sick, stupid, proud, nagging or exhibiting any other fault . . . Consider the food that nourishes the child in his mother's womb. It is evident that the embryo is fed by the menstrual blood; . . . This substance is said to be so detestable and impure that it makes trees barren and vineyards unproductive. It can kill grass and if a dog eats out of it, rabies result. Should the menstrual blood infect the male seed it may cause leprosy and elephantiasis in the child.[37]

Albert the Great, one of the great theologians of the thirteenth century, had a similar problem.

Woman is less qualified [than man] for moral behaviour. For the woman contains more liquid than the man, and it is a property of liquid to take things up easily and to hold onto them poorly. Liquids are easily moved, hence women are inconstant and curious. When a woman has relations with a man, she would like, as much as possible, to be lying with another man at the same time. Woman knows nothing of fidelity. Believe me, if you give her your trust, you will be disappointed. Trust an experienced teacher. For this reason prudent men share their plans and actions least of all with their wives. Woman is a misbegotten man and has a faulty and defective nature in comparison with his. Therefore she is unsure in herself. What she herself cannot get, she seeks to obtain through lying and diabolical deceptions. And so, to put it briefly, one must be on one's guard with every woman, as if she were a poisonous snake and the horned devil . . . In evil and perverse doings woman is cleverer, that is, slyer,

---

37. Pope Innocent III (formerly known as Cardinal Deacon Lotario dei Conti di Segni), *De Contemptu Mundi sive De Miseria Humanae Conditionis Libri Tres*, bk 1 , chs 1–18 . PL vol 217 cols 702–711. Cf *On the Misery of the Human Condition—De Misera Humanae Conditionis*, edited by Donald R Howard, translated by Margaret Mary Dietz (Indianapoos: Bobbs-Merrill, 1969).

than man. Her feelings drive woman toward every evil, just as reason impels man toward all good.[38]

The heretical ideas of the second century Gnostics with their dualistic and pessimistic interpretation of the universe, their contempt for the body and all things material—ideas taken up and preached later by the Manicheans, and later again by the Albigensians or Cathars; the extreme, ascetical practices of monks and hermits from the third century and the strange mentality behind them; the Platonic and neo-Platonic dichotomy between body and soul; the ascetic dictates of Stoicism which floated in the ether breathed by the early Church; St Augustine's attitude to sexual concourse and his theory of original sin being spread like a disease by sexual intercourse; the belief of the early Church that the world was about to end in some general cosmic catastrophe; a emerging fear of women as temptresses, witches and successors of Eve who led Adam astray and upset the spiritual harmony of the world; the development of ascetical, repressive practices to emulate the sufferings of the early martyrs and to chain down the unruly moods and humours; the constant attempts of local councils of bishops to keep their clergy away from women, out of the presbyteries and sacristies, to preserve the accumulating wealth of the Church and enforce the dictates of celibacy—all these ideas and influences have contributed to destroying the creational message of Biblical literature and the fundamental message of the New Testament that the Word of God emptied himself and took on the real form and true character of a flesh man, and resulted in twisting into a tangle any possibility of a healthy theology of sexuality.

Let us pause for a moment to recall just a few *bons mots* of Albert the Great on the subject of sexual activity and its consequences. He thought it was indecent to have sex on Sundays, feast days, on days of fasting and processions (IV sent d 32 a10). Frequent intercourse led to premature ageing and death (de animalibus 1.9 and 15). Too much sex thins out the brain and the indulgent person's eyes sink into their sockets and his eye-sight deteriorates (*Quaestiones super de*

---

38. Albertus Magnus, *Opera Omnia*, tome 12, *Quaestiones super De Animalibus*, XV, q11, edition Coloniensis, published by Monasterii Westfalorum in aedibus Aschendorff, 1951.

animalibus, XV, q 14). Excessive activity causes baldness because sex dries out the body of the participant and cools him out (*Quaestiones super de animalibus* XIX, q 7-9). Being an observant scholar, Albert noticed that those who have sex often are followed around by dogs, because they are attracted by the strong smell of rotten semen (*Quaestiones super de animalibus* V, q 11-14). Let's leave Albert there, on that elevated note.

Our Church has much ground to cover, putrid stables to clean out before she can speak persuasively to the world and to us about the world, about our lives, our bodies and what they are built to do, and about a creator God.

Science and us

While there have been many gifted Christian scholars down the centuries who have shown a marked interest in the scientific world, and not least among them, Cassiodorus Senator (ca 490-593), Boethius (ca 475-ca 526) Isidore of Seville (ca 560-636) and Gerbert of Aurillac, later Pope Sylvester II (ca 940-1003), to mention a handful —in more recent times, science and religion have tossed about like the galleons of the Spaniards against the English, on a turbulent sea. For many years, religion was in the ascendancy and, like a snarling dog, protected its patch savagely. In the late sixteenth century, when the institution and society at large accepted the flat-earth, Ptolemaic view of the universe, Nicolas Copernicus had devised the dangerous hypothesis that the sun was the centre of our solar system. The boys at the Vatican went ahead and listed his publications on the Index of prohibited and dangerous books. A few years before, the zealous fathers of the Inquisition had burnt the scholar and mathematician, Giordano Bruno, in a ceremony conducted on the Campo dei Fiori in Rome.

The Italian astronomer and mathematician, Galileo Galilei, under torture, recanted his silly notion that the earth revolved around the sun. His idea was contrary to the official Ptolemaic belief of the Holy Office, so in lieu of capital punishment, he was condemned to imprisonment as a person 'vehemently suspected of heresy'.

For many centuries, and up to modern times, within living memory, a Christian was not free to believe that Adam and Eve were anything other than our real first parents, or that the world was not created in six days as recorded by the author of Genesis. The diabolical theory of evolution was anathema. All the words of the Bible were to be taken as literally true and scientifically correct.

By its intractability, the blind stupidity of those in charge and their fear of losing control, our Church lost her initiative. Partly because of her arrogant intransigence, many people you meet in the street or see on television confess themselves to be atheists—politicians, novelists, social commentators, singers, actors and scientists—and ordinary people. These people, with impunity and without challenge, feels free to deny the existence of God, to assert that the world and human life have no meaning or purpose, that any religious belief is incompatible with the secular sciences, and plainly ridiculous.

Our Church had for generations busied herself with, and claimed dominion over matters that had nothing to do with her. She had seen enemies where there were only shadows and figments of fear. She had made loud dogmatic pronouncements when all she had to do was look, listen quietly and learn. She could not imagine that religion and science belonged to two different worlds. Science functioned in the world of observable, tangible realities and based its findings on the laws of probability. Religion functions in the sphere of the spiritual, the unseen, in the world of mystery and imagination, of poetry and metephor. While science relies on experiment and measurement, religion depends on intuition, on the experience of love, joy, sorrow, loss, of transcendence, faithfulness—matters about which science can have nothing meaningful to say. Science is cold, calculating and rational, whereas religion is a matter of the heart. They live and flourish in two separate stratospheres. The rules that regulate the world of science should not be forced into service in the other world—and vice versa. Religion is a search to uncover the meaning and purpose of our existence and of our universe, whereas science attempts, by hypotheses, testing and retesting, to find out how our universe and how our bodies work.

Our Catholic Church, being an essentially religious institution, devalued her currency by continually overstepping the mark and making claims well outside her area of competence. At one stage, she thought she ruled the world, and in the process, she became an organisation with a reputation of being hostile to the scientific world —its values and methods. Consequently, many Christians believed they were condemned to function in two separate worlds which could not communicate one with the other, that faith was doomed to be a schizophrenic experience in the modern world. And many secular, modern citizens simply assume that religion and science cannot stand each other, cannot be seen in the same room, and that when religion challenges science to a duel, science easily dispatched her bullying antagonist.

These attitudes have to change, our institution has to change—for the survival of the Church, and so that the lives of men and women can be enriched and their spiritual thirst quenched.

In harmony with the principles and values of the fathers of Vatican II in *Gaudium et Spes*, we have to read the signs of the times, learn to dialogue with the modern world and find ways to embrace the discoveries of the secular sciences. What we certainly didn't need in Sydney was a cardinal who turned his back on the scientific world, as Rome insisted on doing from the sixteenth to the beginning of the twentieth century, and denying, against the best scientific data interpreted by the best scientific brains, that the potentially tragic effects of climate change are man-made and must be rectified with all speed and whatever the cost. The end result was that our Church became, once again, a relic from the dark side, and a figure of fun. Fortunately, we now have a pope with a university degree in science.

Talking among ourselves

Enough of the challenges issued by the modern world to some of the basic beliefs and attitudes in the life of the Church. Let us turn inwards and talk among ourselves about the institution and its internal processes which, in my opinion, must change, and eventually will change. Let us accept with a peaceful mind that there can be no change without deviation, without dissent and disagreement, and sometimes without a team of revolting prophets. I do not feel the need to expand on my suggestions since, as far as I am concerned, they are simple statements of the 'bleeding obvious', and if you don't agree, the only conclusion I can reasonably draw is that we are living on alien planets.

I am in favour of—

Finding a new, contemporary way of selecting and installing a successor of Peter the Apostle, the bishop of Rome, as the head of the episcopal college. A secret conclave of papal appointees to the exclusive rank of eminent princes, with white smoke dribbling out of the Vatican chimney only reminds me of Dorothy exposing the wizard of Oz at the end of the yellow brick road. Some enjoy the drama and the spendour of a papal election. Personally, I think it verges on being superstitious and ridiculous. A more inclusive and democratic way could, and should be devised to ensure that the man in charge truly emerges from the ranks of the People of God. Over the centuries, the Spirit has worked in many differing ways and through many inadequate agents to select a successor of Peter, and there is no good reason why she cannot do so again. The present process is too clerical, too opaque, too rarified, and the team of candidates too homogenised and Vaticanised.

I am in favour of—

Finding a new way of selecting a bishop for a local diocese. Judas' successor to the Apostolic College was selected on the throw of a dice. Even when autocratic and monarchical governance was the *secular* norm, the Church's method of episcopal selection remained in the hands of local or regional leaders and citizens. Sometimes laypeople or deacons were chosen by popular acclaim to be the bishop. All the faithful members should have some real part in the selection of their bishop. The process does not have to be secret, or carried out in the shadowy corridors of some distant bureaucracy. An archbishop should not be appointed to a diocese in the dead of night. In the modern world, involvement, participation and transparency have a certain attraction.

I am in favour of—

Parishioners having a significant vote in the appointment of their parish priest. It's no longer good enough that this power of appointment is left to the whim of the bishop acting at a distance, in secret and without proper consultation. Baptism and grace give the members of the People of God the right to be involved in the life of the Church, and the duty to participate. The members should have a say. They should not continue to be treated with such disrespect.

I am in favour of—

Establishing an up-to-date, rigorous, highly professional program of training and educating those who decide to present themselves for priestly ministry. There can be no real, radical reform of the institution until its religious leaders and ministers are properly educated for their life in the modern world.

I am in favour of—

Establishing a system for the training and ordination of worldly-wise married men to work in parishes.

I am in favour of—

Restricting the reception of a candidate for Holy Orders into a formal training program until he has lived a life somewhere in the world, made mistakes and proven himself a mature and balanced member of society. The minimum age of entry should be between thirty and thirty-five. Experience has shown that it's crazy to require a young man to seclude himself from the world for seven or more years, to ordain him at the age of twenty-three or twenty-four and expect him to function for the rest of his life without experieincing serious personal problems.

I am in favour of—

Serious consideration being given to establishing a temporary priestly ministry for, say seven years, with the possibility of a re-committment for further periods.

I am in favour of—

Priesthood (and by necessary implication, episcopacy and papacy) being open to any member of the Christian community over a certain age, given the requisite level of faith and maturity—black or white, rich or poor, Jew or gentile, male or female, straight or gay.

I am in favour of—

The ordination of women so that they too can exercise a public ministry of teaching, of celebrating the mysteries of the Eucharist and of mediating God's mercy in the sacrament of forgiveness. Have you observed, have the members of the men's club in the Vatican noticed that half the population on earth is female. Women are bus-drivers, police officers, soldiers, politicians, doctors, researchers, lawyers, barristers, judges, bankers, poets, radio-presenters, film directors, journalists and engineers. Hillary Clinton, Angela Merkel, Condolesa Rice, Mary Robinson, Nancy Pilosa, Julia Gillard, Quentin Bryce, Heather Ridout, Maria Bashiar—Do I need to go on?

I am in favour of –

New ministries being developed and ceremonies devised for proper induction—ministries of the sick, for prisoners, for funerals, for the poor, catechists, liturgists etc.

I am in favour of—

Doing away with titular bishoprics which attract merely honorific ranks and, if necessary, of expanding the ranks of monsignors.

The question of an evangelical return to the dictates of simplicity and to the embrace of the poor is critical to our Church as she seeks to engage in dialogue with the modern world. At the first session of the Second Vatican Council, on 6 December 1962, the observations and recommendations of Cardinal Giacomo Lercaro of Bologna were applauded by bishops and cardinals from around the world. Speaking of the mystery of Christ in the poor, he made the following suggestions—

1. Before all else, the Church should present the doctrine of the poverty of Christ. This would involve the presentation of an infant born of a humble Jewish girl somewhere in the backblocks of the Roman Empire; his simple lifestyle with his

companions on the road; his death as a common criminal; his association with the poor, with sinners and tax-collectors; the Pauline teaching of the Word emptying himself to take on the form of a man, and humbling himself to die on a cross.
2. In its teaching and in its daily life, the Church should give priority to the evangelical doctrine of the eminent dignity of the poor. This is a counter-intuitive, and a radically counter-cultural position which should amaze the world.
3. The Church should develop the link between Christ's presence in the poor and his hidden presence in the Eucharist and in an impoverished hierarchy.
4. The Church should place limits on the use it makes of material wealth, and on episcopal pomp. On this subject, no more need by said.
5. The Church must embrace a new economic order—restraint, austerity, fairness, equality, justice for all.[39]

And if I might be permitted a personal observation, on the high standard recommended by Cardinal Lercaro, the Vatican would fail miserably. Zero out of ten. And an archdiocese situated in the advanced economies such as Sydney, would score marginally better—perhaps three out of ten. In marking a prosperous local diocese, I would be taking in consideration the Christmas tree in the churches, the work of the St Vincent de Paul society, the religious sisters' hidden service to the poor, to the sick and dying, the work of chaplains to prisons. But the overall impression given off by the institution is one of wealth and extravagance, of comfort, large buildings and expensive robes. And Jesus weeps.

You might think that all or some of these recommended institutional changes might offend the basic principles on which our Church has been founded, and survived for over two millennia. Personally, I do not see any theological barrier to the implementation of any one of these recommendations—and many more. Until recent times, the Church has been able to change and adapt, and has done so radically over the centuries, ever since the apostolic meeting in Jerusalem in about 50 AD. For the sake of the Gospel and to continue its mission, she must do so again—rapidly, radically.

---

39. Yves Congar, *My Journal of the Council*, 241

On Tuesday 3 December 1963, the Council Fathers and Pope Paul VI assembled in St Peter's to commemorate the fourth centenary of the Council of Trent. In the course of the ceremony, the pope read the *motu proprio Pastorale Munus*. Yves Congar was saddened by the recent death of his mother and by the slow progress being made at the Council in Rome. He was extremely unwell, and conscious that many hours of his valuable time was being wasted. Probably the most influential peritus at the Council was an impatient, cranky man.

'What a frightful thing Rome is, reducing everything to ceremonies.'[40]

By Tuesday 26 October 1965, the Council was slowly grinding to an end. Congar wrote so hopefully, so optimistically in his personal journal—

> Little by little we are escaping from Pius IX and Pius XII (I mention these here only from the point of view of their refusal of the world as it is). Everything is cohering: the world of the Council is extraordinarily coherent. The page is being turned over on Augustinianism and on the Middle Ages. Pretensions to temporal power are being renounced. New structures of relationship with the world are being put in place, beginning from the Gospel and in the light of Jesus Christ . . .[41]

Reflecting earlier on the proceedings in the Vatican on 3 December 1963, Congar wrote in his Journal—

> But I am more and more struck by the fact that all that is very much among ourselves. And that it has little or no contact with the real world. These are disputes between clerics, as in the fifteenth century. There ought to be contact with real men and women, with a real world! We produce paper, make speeches, and then what?
>
> In the end, a list was read this morning of the faculties that the pope grants to bishops: '*concedimus*' (we grant), '*impertimur*' (we impart). Whereas, in reality, all he is doing is to give back—and not graciously!—a part of what had been stolen from them over the centuries!!![42]

---

40. Yves Congar, *My Journal of the Council*, 457.
41. Yves Congar, *My Journal of the Council*, 825–56.
42. Yves Congar, *My Journal of the Council*, 465.

Two years before, on 10 March 1961, during the preparation for the Council, Congar had received a letter from François Tollu, the superior of the Séminaire de Carmes at the Institut Catholique in Paris, telling him that Cardinal Guiseppe Pizzardo had forbidden the publication and use in the seminary of a theological manual written in the French language. Teaching in the seminary had to be conducted in Latin. The professors were forbidden to use modern languages.

Cardinal Pizzardo was the prefect of the Congregation for Seminaries and Universities, and later became the president of the conciliar Commission on Seminaries, Studies, and Catholic Education.

After receiving the Tollu letter, Congar wrote—

> I really think that the French bishops ought to go ahead and ignore the senile threats of an idiot.[43]

In a later journal entry, he described Pizzardo as an 'imbecile'.[44] åAnyway, he wrote back to Tollu, observing that Latin was one of the means by which people seek to cling to the structures of influence which are associated with the posts they occupy. He observed that in Rome there was a reactionary and stupidly narrow clique which was trying to keep the windows closed. The future cardinal concluded his letter with this disturbing observation—

> There is no sin in recovering a freedom that has been stolen.[45]

---

43. Yves Congar, *My Journal of the Council*, 43.
44. Yves Congar, *My Journal of the Council*, 465.
45. Yves Congar, *My Journal of the Coucil*, 43.

Good News and Bad News in the Church

Fr Frank Brennan SJ

Good news: new pope; Bad news: sexual abuse

At my regular parish mass in Canberra on the Fifth Sunday of Lent just after the election of our new pope, I recall greeting the congregation with these words: 'Good evening. My name is Frank and I am a Jesuit. I've had a good week. I hope you have too.' I have been overwhelmed by the positive response by all sorts of people to the election of the first Jesuit pope. I have happily received the congratulations without quite knowing what to do with them, nor what I did to deserve them! It is still early days in his pontificate, but I think he has opened up a vast new panacea and not just for Catholics. Francis is theologically orthodox, politically conservative, comfortable in his own skin, infectiously pastoral, and truly committed to the poor. Of late, most thinking Catholics engaged in the world have wondered how you could possibly be theologically orthodox and infectiously pastoral at the one time, how you could be politically conservative and still have a commitment to the poor, how you could be comfortable in your own skin—at ease in Church and in the public square, equally comfortable and uncomfortable in conversation with fawning devotees and hostile critics. Think only of Francis's remark during the press conference on the plane on the way back from World Youth Day: 'If a person is gay and seeks the Lord and has good will, who am I to judge him?'[1] Gone are the days of rainbow sashes outside Cathedrals and threats of communion bans.

As Francis says in the lengthy interview he did for the Jesuit journal *La Civilta Cattolica* in September 2013: 'We need to proclaim the Gospel on every street corner, preaching the good news of the

---

1. *The Tablet*, 3 August 2013, 31.

kingdom and healing, even with our preaching, every kind of disease and wound. In Buenos Aires I used to receive letters from homosexual persons who are "socially wounded" because they tell me that they feel like the church has always condemned them."[2] In that interview he recalls:

> A person once asked me, in a provocative manner, if I approved of homosexuality. I replied with another question: 'Tell me: when God looks at a gay person, does he endorse the existence of this person with love, or reject and condemn this person?' We must always consider the person. Here we enter into the mystery of the human being. In life, God accompanies persons, and we must accompany them, starting from their situation. It is necessary to accompany them with mercy. When that happens, the Holy Spirit inspires the priest to say the right thing.[3]

Here is a pope who is not just about creating wiggle room or watering down the teachings of the Church. No, he wants to admit honestly to the world that we hold in tension definitive teachings and pastoral yearnings—held together coherently only by mercy and forgiveness.

He explains:

> We cannot insist only on issues related to abortion, gay marriage and the use of contraceptive methods. This is not possible. I have not spoken much about these things, and I was reprimanded for that. But when we speak about these issues, we have to talk about them in a context. The teaching of the church, for that matter, is clear and I am a son of the church, but it is not necessary to talk about these issues all the time. The dogmatic and moral teachings of the church are not all equivalent. The church's pastoral ministry cannot be obsessed with the transmission of a disjointed multitude of doctrines to be imposed insistently. Proclamation in a missionary style focuses on the essentials, on the necessary things: this is also what fascinates and attracts more, what makes the heart burn, as it did for the disciples at Emmaus. We have to find a new balance; otherwise even the moral edifice of the church is

---

2. *America*, 30 September 2013, 24.
3. *America*, 30 September 2013. 26.

likely to fall like a house of cards, losing the freshness and fragrance of the Gospel. The proposal of the Gospel must be more simple, profound, radiant. It is from this proposition that the moral consequences then flow.[4]

If we are honest with ourselves, many of us have wondered how we can maintain our Christian faith and our commitment at this time in the Catholic Church in the wake of the sexual abuse crisis and the many judgmental utterances about sexuality and reproduction. The Church that has spoken longest and loudest about sex in all its modalities seems to be one of the social institutions most needing to get its own house in order in relation to trust, fidelity, love, respect and human dignity. Revelations out of Melbourne, Ballarat and Newcastle and the pending national royal commission hearings leave us with heavy hearts especially about some of our local church leadership before 1996. But we do have a spring in our step that this new Pope, together with rigorous, independent legal processes (even in the face of much media pre-judgment) and local church commitments to transparency and solicitous care of victims, including the establishment of the Truth Justice and Healing Council, provide us with the structures and leadership necessary for 'cooperation, openness, full disclosure and justice for victims and survivors'[5]. The chief Christian paradox is that we are lowly sinners who dare to profess the highest ideals, and that sometimes we cannot do it on our own—we need the help of our critics and the State. Our greatest possibilities are born of the promise of forgiveness and redemption, the hope of new life emerging from suffering and even death. Out of our past failings and our present shame can come future promise and hope.

Let's be in no doubt that the Australian Catholic Church needed help from the State and from civil society so that we might get our house in order in dealing with child abuse which had been occurring at a most unacceptable rate and which had been addressed in too incremental a way. The royal commission established by the Gillard government is a very cumbersome device for dealing with the matter within the Australian federation. The commission needed a new generation of political patrons even before it began its public

---

4. *America*, 30 September 2013.
5. See http://tjhcouncil.org.au/

hearings. Its remit is impossibly broad. Like the Royal Commission into Aboriginal Deaths in Custody it is pursuing many tracks of academic research but the real test will be its capacity to provide satisfaction to victims and the reassurance to the community that institutional responses have been improved as best they might.

For the Catholic Church, this commission will continue to be a difficult exercise, in part because of the bias of some of the media and some of the key actors—for example, the Victorian Police Force whose performance before the Victorian parliamentary inquiry was a partisan disgrace providing a submission 'limited to comment regarding religious organisations, in particular the Catholic Church', and described by Peter O'Callaghan QC as 'plainly wrong and seriously misconceived'[6], and Newcastle's Inspector Peter Fox who allowed his personal crusade to displace his usual obligations as a police officer.[7] But over time, we should be confident that the truth

---

6. Peter O'Callaghan QC told the Victorian Inquiry on 30 April 2013 at p 3, "Contrary to what the true position is, the relationship which I had enjoyed with the police up until the police submission was received was highly courteous and cooperative, and I trust it still will be. I must say that it came as a complete surprise the volte-face that the police submission and Ashton represented. There are suggestions in the police submission that there was a lack of engagement with the police, and I dispute that. I dispute it from its inception in 1996 when the terms of reference were being promulgated. I think contemporaneously or perhaps a little bit after I was appointed we consulted with Assistant Commissioner Gavin Brown as to the terms of reference. Likewise, those terms of reference were submitted to the then solicitor-general, the late Douglas Graham, and he provided them to members of Parliament et cetera. I discussed it with him. That was the inception. We acted in consultation with the police. Over the years I have had contact with the police. Contrary to what is said—that I have not referred complaints—the fact is that I facilitated the referral of complaints by speaking to victims, telling them of their right to report their complaint to the police and encouraging them to exercise the right. In a number of cases a lot of them still did not want to go to the police, but in a lot of cases—this will appear in some of these exhibits—I rang the relevant police officer and said, 'I have Mr So-and-So here, and he wants to make a complaint'. I then arranged for him to go there."

7. See for example, Dan Box, 'The Fox and his quarry', *The Australian*, 2 August 2013:

   From the start, Fox has cast the entire process as a confrontation between himself and his employer. A day before his first public appearance in the witness box, he tweeted: "I'd rather be on my side this week than NSW Police."

will out. We should have faith that the individual commissioners and the commission's processes will accord natural justice to all, including the Catholic Church. We should accept that our processes pre-1988 were grossly deficient, and that pre-1996 we were on a steep learning curve, and that there are still lessons to learn. We should accept that the common law will be developed in Australia as it has been in Canada and the UK ensuring that the victims of child abuse in institutions will be able to claim the vicarious liability of those employers and institutional managers for the abuse perpetrated in circumstances where employees or religious personnel are standing *in loco parentis* and that employers will be personally liable for their failures adequately to screen, supervise and investigate staff who have ready access to children. It is high time for church employers and institutional owners to assure victims that they will have access to a nominal defendant backed by church resources for discharging direct and vicarious tortious liability for church personnel who should have done better.

Strangely, for a witness, he continues to tweet, and not always accurately, from inside the courtroom itself, provoking criticism from Cunneen.

'It is indecorous conduct, it is undignified conduct. Perhaps it would be better . . . if your time was spent listening to the evidence than suggesting it improperly,' she said.

The detective also has built relationships with many in the press, sitting with reporters during hearings, exchanging text messages and, in their private conversations, accusing other senior police of being criminals themselves.

These claims, like much of Fox's evidence to the inquiry, appear to be unsupported by the facts.

A brief of evidence he claimed to have prepared about one Catholic bishop doesn't exist, the inquiry heard. A computer disk containing a witness statement he claimed to have sent to the NSW Ombudsman cannot be found within their files.

A conversation in which he claimed another policeman warned him about a 'Catholic mafia' within the police is comprehensively denied. 'Evidence' he told Lateline had been destroyed by priests is not evidence at all. It was pornography, the inquiry heard, embarrassing but legal, and without a proven link to any crime.

Despite what media commentators like David Marr have been arguing, the contentious legal issue is not the need to incorporate the Catholic Church as if it were the only Church in Australia immune from suit. The key legal issue is determining the liability of the Church for the criminal wrongs committed by individuals while being employed by the Church or while holding themselves out as acting in the name of the Church. If liable, members of the church or any other unincorporated association under Church auspices need to access property owned by the church property trust for the purposes of paying damages in relation to (a) vicarious liability for criminal wrongdoing of church members; (b) direct liability for church leaders negligently failing to screen, scrutinise and sack offenders; and (c) strict liability of a church conducting an enterprise where the risk to vulnerable children is so self-evident as to warrant strict liability.

The Royal Commission will come and go. Some changes will be made to the law. But in the end, the issue will not be law and media perceptions of the Catholic Church. The issue will be our capacity as Church to put vulnerable children at the centre as did Jesus and to put behind us the clericalist mindset which put the institution, its status and wealth at the centre as did our hierarchy for too long.

Good news: forgiveness and reconciliation; Bad news: hierarchy and clericalism

Something crystallised for me at an appearance in March 2014 at the Opera House with the British philosopher A C Grayling, author of *The God Argument*, and Sean Faircloth, a US director of one of the Dawkins Institutes passionately committed to atheism. We were there to discuss their certainty about the absurdity of religious faith. Mr Faircloth raised what has already become a hoary old chestnut, the failure of Pope Francis when provincial of the Jesuits in Argentina during the Dirty Wars to adequately defend his fellow Jesuits who were detained and tortured by unscrupulous soldiers. Being a Jesuit, I thought I was peculiarly well situated to respond. I confess to having got a little carried away. I exclaimed: Yes, how much better it would have been if there had been just one secular, humanist, atheist philosopher who had stood up in the city square in Buenos Aires and shouted, 'Stop it!' The military junta would have collectively come to their senses, stopped it, and Argentinians would have lived happily ever after. The luxury for such philosophers is that they never have to get their hands dirty and they think that religious people who do are hypocrites unless of course they take the course of martyrdom. It's only as Church that I think we can hold together ideals and reality, commitment and forgiveness.

Before we canonise Francis too quickly, let's concede that he was a divisive figure in his home province of Argentina when was made Jesuit Provincial at the age of only 36. The *Tablet* has carried extracts from Paul Vallely's new book *Pope Francis: Untying the Knots* which includes the explosive email sent by one of the serving Jesuit provincials in another Latin American country when Bergoglio's election was announced in St Peter's Square. This Jesuit provincial wrote:

> Yes I know Bergoglio. He's a person who's caused a lot of problems in the Society and is highly controversial in his own country. In addition to being accused of having allowed the arrest of two Jesuits during the time of the Argentinian dictatorship, as provincial he generated divided loyalties: some groups almost worshipped him, while others would have nothing to do with him, and he would hardly speak to them. It was an absurd situation. He is well-trained and very capable, but is surrounded by this personality cult which is extremely divisive. He has an aura of spirituality which he uses to obtain power. It will be a catastrophe for the Church to have someone like him in the Apostolic See. He left the Society of Jesus in Argentina destroyed with Jesuits divided and institutions destroyed and financially broken. We have spent two decades trying to fix the chaos that the man left us.[8]

Like all of us, Francis has feet of clay; he is a sinner; there are things in his past that he regrets. As Francis himself now admits: 'My style of government as a Jesuit at the beginning had many faults. That was a difficult time for the Society: an entire generation of Jesuits had disappeared. Because of this I found myself provincial when I was still very young. I was only 36 years old. That was crazy. I had

---

8. *The Tablet*, 10 August 2013, p 4.

to deal with difficult situations, and I made my decisions abruptly and by myself.⁹ He is a man who has learnt much by his mistakes; he is a sinner who has grown and thrived through his experience of the Lord's mercy. As he says, 'My authoritarian and quick manner of making decisions led me to have serious problems and to be accused of being ultraconservative. I lived a time of great interior crisis when I was in Cordova. To be sure, I have never been like Blessed Imelda [a goody-goody], but I have never been a right-winger. It was my authoritarian way of making decisions that created problems. I say these things from life experience and because I want to make clear what the dangers are. Over time I learned many things. The Lord has allowed this growth in knowledge of government through my faults and my sins.'¹⁰ What a Jesuit; what a Pope; what a man!

There are many things that his erstwhile critics regret. Having fallen out with many Jesuits in his home province, he enjoyed the favour of Pope John Paul II. There were tensions between him and Fr Pedro Arrupe, the Superior General of the Jesuits at the time of the Jesuit General Congregations which defined the Jesuit mission in terms of faith AND justice. The greatness of Francis has been in his capacity to transcend these differences and to be gracious even to those opposed to his viewpoints after many years of silence and isolation. It was very heartening for Jesuits of all stripes to learn of Francis's Mass at the Gesu Church in Rome on the Feast of St Ignatius on 31 July 2013. He visited the tomb of Pedro Arrupe. Just as he had mentioned Matteo Ricci and Karl Rahner in his earlier visit to the offices of *La Civilta Cattolica*¹¹, he mentioned Francis Xavier and Pedro Arrupe in his homily at the Gesu—each time linking an historic and contemporary figure, and each time the contemporary figure being one who had difficult relations with the Vatican from time to time. It's a long time since any Pope mentioned Karl Rahner or Pedro Arrupe in a positive light. In his homily for the feast of St Ignatius, Francis said:

---

9. *America*, 30 September 2013, p 20.
10. Ibid.
11. Pope Francis, *Address To The Community Of Writers Of 'La Civiltà Cattolica'*, 14 June 2013. See http://www.vatican.va/holy_father/francesco/speeches/2013/june/documents/papa-francesco_20130614_la-civilta-cattolica_en.html

> I have always liked to dwell on the twilight of a Jesuit, when a Jesuit is nearing the end of life, on when he is setting. And two images of this Jesuit twilight always spring to mind: a classical image, that of St Francis Xavier looking at China. Art has so often depicted this passing, Xavier's end. So has literature, in that beautiful piece by Pemán. At the end, without anything but before the Lord; thinking of this does me good. The other sunset, the other image that comes to mind as an example is that of Fr Arrupe in his last conversation in the refugee camp, when he said to us—something he used to say—'I say this as if it were my swan song: pray'. Prayer, union with Jesus. Having said these words he took the plane to Rome and upon arrival suffered a stroke that led to the sunset—so long and so exemplary—of his life. Two sunsets, two images, both of which it will do us all good to look at and to return to. And we should ask for the grace that our own passing will resemble theirs.[12]

As Catholics we can bring God's blessings to all in our world, even those who have no time for our Church and not much interest in our Lord. Remember how Pope Francis ended his address to the journalists in Rome providing a blessing with a difference. He said:

> I told you I was cordially imparting my blessing. Since many of you are not members of the Catholic Church, and others are not believers, I cordially give this blessing silently, to each of you, respecting the conscience of each, but in the knowledge that each of you is a child of God. May God bless you![13]

Now that's what I call a real blessing for journalists—and not a word of Vaticanese. Respect for the conscience of every person, regardless of their religious beliefs; silence in the face of difference; affirmation of the dignity and blessedness of every person; offering, not coercing; suggesting, not dictating; leaving room for gracious acceptance. These

---

12. Pope Francis, *Homily*, Church of Gesu, 31 July 2013.
    See http://www.vatican.va/holy_father/francesco/homilies/2013/documents/papa-francesco_20130731_omelia-sant-ignazio_en.html
13. Pope Francis, *Audience with Media Representatives*, 16 March 2013. See http://www.vatican.va/holy_father/francesco/speeches/2013/march/documents/papa-francesco_20130316_rappresentanti-media_en.html

are all good pointers for us Catholics helping to form the Church of the 21ˢᵗ century holding the treasure of tradition, authority and ritual in trust for all the people of God, including your children and grandchildren, as we discern how best to make a home for God in our lives and in our world, assured that the Spirit of God has made her home with us.

We Catholics know that any spirituality worth its salt needs the buttress of authority, tradition, ritual and community. Many Catholics understandably have become so despairing of the Church or so entranced with the post-modern world, that they think they will just have to make do with a combination of homespun spirituality and a grounded secular commitment to justice. The American theologian Sandra Marie Schneiders puts it this way:

> Postmodernity is characterised by fragmentation of thought and experience which focuses attention on the present moment, on immediate satisfaction, on what works for me rather than on historical continuity, social consensus, or shared hopes for a common future. In this foundationless, relativistic, and alienated context there is, nevertheless, often a powerfully experienced need for some focus of meaning, some source of direction and value. The intense interest in spirituality today is no doubt partially an expression of this need. Religion, however, especially the type to which Christianity belongs, presupposes a unitary worldview whose master narrative stretching from creation to the end of the world is ontologically based and which makes claims to universal validity while promising an eschatological reward for delayed personal gratification and sacrificial social commitment. In other words, the Christian religion is intrinsically difficult to reconcile with a postmodern sensibility. By contrast, a non-religious spirituality is often very compatible with that sensibility precisely because it is usually a privatised, idiosyncratic, personally satisfying stance and practice which makes no doctrinal claims, imposes no moral authority outside one's own conscience, creates no necessary personal relationships or social responsibilities, and can be

> changed or abandoned whenever it seems not to work for the practitioner. Commitment, at least of any relatively permanent kind, which involves both an implied affirmation of personal subjectivity and a conviction about cosmic objectivity, is easily circumvented by a spirituality which has no institutional or community affiliation. Clearly such a spirituality is much more compatible with a postmodern sensibility than the religion of any church, especially Christianity.[14]

All parishioners are wrestling with the great paradoxes of modern life. Talk of 'a unitary worldview', 'a master narrative', 'universal validity', 'eschatological reward' seems so paradoxical— talk which is seemingly self-contradictory or absurd but in reality expressing a possible truth, all the more ineffable when we gather amongst like-minded friends with a touch of cynicism about our local church hierarchy wondering where all this Francis business is leading or when it will end. I was dumbfounded when I completed an interview on ABC PM about Francis's interview released that day by *La Civilta Cattolica*. The story ended with the observation by the reporter: 'PM contacted the Archbishops of Brisbane, Sydney and Tasmania, however all declined to comment.'[15] Cardinal Pell issued a statement hosing down the excitement about Francis's own interview. His statement commenced: 'Two paragraphs in Pope Francis' important 12,000 word interview have been the focus of particular attention. He also emphasised the importance of not taking issues out of context.'[16] I was rather more taken with the statement released by Cardinal Dolan in New York affirming that Francis's interview 'confirms what has been apparent during these first six months of his papacy: that he is a man who profoundly believes in the mercy of a loving God, and who wants to bring that message of mercy to the entire world, including

---

14. Sandra Marie Schneiders, 'Religion vs Spirituality: A Contemporary Conundrum', *Spiritus: A Journal of Christian Spirituality*, Volume 3, Number 2, Fall 2003, pp 163-185 at p 173.
15. ABC *PM*, 20 September 2013. See http://www.abc.net.au/pm/content/2013/s3853481.htm. Archbishop Colerridge later told me that he would have been delighted to comment but was unavailable.
16. Cardinal George Pell, Media Statement, 20 September 2013 now reported at http://www.sydneycatholic.org/news/latest_news/2013/2013920_354.shtml

those who feel that they have been wounded by the Church. As a priest and bishop, I particularly welcome his reminder that the clergy are primarily to serve as shepherds, to be with our people, to walk with them, to be pastors, not bureaucrats!'[17]

So many of our personal dealings within the Church are restricted by old time hierarchical and clerical notions. A while ago I wrote a lengthy letter to a bishop explaining why I disagreed with his public statements on same sex marriage and civil unions. He never even acknowledged the letter. Next time we met socially, it was a case of 'Don't mention the war.' It's clear. He's a bishop; I'm not. No correspondence will be entered into. How are we to formulate credible arguments in the square of a pluralistic democratic society when we don't even talk to each other? A month or two later, I was convinced by the secretariat of the bishops' conference to appear on television to discuss same sex marriage because none of the twelve bishops approached was available.

Good news: variety in a broad Church; Bad news: acute shortage of priests and religious

A broad church we need to be gentle, encouraging and accommodating of each other, as well as firm, demanding and accountable. You could hear it in the tension around the table at Geraldine Doogue's ABC Compass dinner in October 2013 with Chris Geraghty, ex-priest, retired judge and North Sydney parishioner, and Mary Clare Meney, mother of nine and Co-ordinator of the National Association of Catholic Families, discussing why they are still Catholic. Here is some of the dialogue:[18]

Chris
I love to just sit in the presence of the transcendent but I can't tell you —and I think this is the big challenge the church has now in this age of atheism—to tell the world something, anything, about God.

---

17. Cardinal Timothy Dolan, Media Statement, 19 September 2013 available at http://www.archny.org/news-events/news-press-releases/index.cfm?i=30736
18. ABC TV, *Compass*, 29 September 2013. Transcript at http://www.abc.net.au/compass/s3840716.htm

To put some kind of image on it. And my image comes from Jesus, who I regard as a deeply, deeply troubling religious person who challenged the society and who criticised it, who was countercultural, who was rebellious. He was really profoundly disturbing. He wasn't the sacred heart. He wasn't meek and mild. He was just an ordinary person and Mary his mother, was just an ordinary, fairly uneducated we think, teenager who accepted the grace of God.

And we've changed that into—excuse me but—our Lady of Lourdes for example. We're kind of surrounded by all this—I think—pagan paraphernalia.

Geraldine Doogue
Well I'm thinking Mary-Clare you would have some different needs to Chris wouldn't you?

Mary-Clare
Of course. It's not about needs. It's about the four kinds of prayer, which is about faith but it's also . . . we don't just talk to someone when we need something. Its love, adoration, petition, sorrow for our sins. We sin all the time.

Chris
No we don't! I do not.

Mary-Clare
Well I do. Perhaps you don't. (laughs)

Chris
No. But you don't either.

Mary-Clare
Oh no, no. I've been told that before. I don't believe it. Sorry.

In his 2013 address to the Brazilian bishops, Pope Francis warned that we must not yield to the fear once expressed by Blessed John Henry Newman that 'the Christian world is gradually becoming barren and effete, as land which has been worked out and is become sand'. Francis said, 'We must not yield to disillusionment, discouragement and complaint. We have laboured greatly and, at times, we see what appear to be failures. We feel like those who must tally up a losing season as we consider those who have left us or no longer consider us credible or relevant.'[19]

Francis drew upon one of his favourite gospel scenes, Luke's account of the disillusioned disciples on the Road to Emmaus failing to recognise the one who broke open the scriptures to them, then recognising him belatedly in the breaking of the bread:

> Here we have to face the difficult mystery of those people who leave the Church, who, under the illusion of alternative ideas, now think that the Church—their Jerusalem—can no longer offer them anything meaningful and important. So they set off on the road alone, with their disappointment. Perhaps the Church appeared too weak, perhaps too distant from their needs, perhaps too poor to respond to their concerns, perhaps too cold, perhaps too caught up with itself, perhaps a prisoner of its own rigid formulas, perhaps the world seems to have made the Church a relic of the past, unfit for new questions; perhaps the Church could speak to people in their infancy but not to those come of age.[20]

Asking what then are we to do, Francis answers:

> We need a Church unafraid of going forth into **their** night. We need a Church capable of meeting them on **their** way. We need a Church capable of entering into **their** conversation. We need a Church able to dialogue with those disciples who, having left Jerusalem behind, are wandering aimlessly, alone, with their own disappointment, disillusioned by a Christianity now considered barren, fruitless soil, incapable of generating meaning.[21]

I caused alarm with some of my fellow Jesuits a while ago when I gave an interview to *The Good Weekend* magazine in the *Sydney Morning Herald* saying: 'I wouldn't be a priest if I was 21 today. I am one of the last generations of Irish Catholics whose families made it

---

19. Address of Pope Francis, *Meeting with Bishops of Brazil*, 28 July 2013, at http://www.vatican.va/holy_father/francesco/speeches/2013/july/documents/papa-francesco_20130727_gmg-episcopato-brasile_en.html
20. Address of Pope Francis, *Meeting with Bishops of Brazil*.
21. Address of Pope Francis, *Meeting with Bishops of Brazil*.

professionally and were comfortable with the church. I love being a Jesuit but I can't honestly say I would join now. My religious faith has remained rock solid, but there are times when I feel really cheesed off with the institutional church, which sometimes treats its lay members and non-members in a too-patronising fashion."[22]

When I joined the Jesuits, approximately 25 per cent of clerical religious were 60 or over, with very few aged 75 or over. More than one-third (36.6%) were under the age of 40, with 9.8 per cent under 25 years. By 2009, only 10 per cent of clerical religious were under 40, with just 0.7 per cent aged under 25. That's an enormous challenge for a 21 year old.

As I have said to my superiors, we need to see how a young man might discern that action of the Spirit in calling him to a group which is aged and diminished, though armed with a fine founding charism and recent documents which make for splendid reading in terms of mission and life. For example, if I were contemplating priesthood, the diaconate or religious life aged 21 today and was attracted to the Australian Jesuits, I would need to consider some additional factors which were not relevant in 1975: I will be responsible in fraternal charity for a disproportionate number of my brothers who are retired and moving towards death; I will not be accompanied by a significant number of like-minded contemporaries; I will be expected to oversee corporate enterprises boasting the Ignatian charism with a reduced expectation that I will have a long working life largely dedicated just to learning, teaching or direct pastoral involvement—I will be expected to serve on various boards safeguarding the charism of the organisation being run by competent lay people many of whom go home to their spouse and children at night. And I will be part of an apostolic group dedicated to the universal mission of the Church but with few inspiring demands or expressions of trust from the local hierarchy. For example I was adviser to the Australian Catholic Bishops on the contested issue of Aboriginal rights at the age of 30. It would be unimaginable nowadays that the Bishops Conference would commission a 30-year-old priest or religious to perform such a task in the public square. The Spirit may still be calling me but not in the same exciting and challenging way that the Spirit would have been calling the same young man had he turned 21 in 1975 rather than 2015.

---

22. *Sydney Morning Herald*, Good Weekend, 28 May 2011, p 30.

After my *Good Weekend* Interview, one very fine Jesuit wrote to me saying:

> A vocation to the priesthood is basically a particular relationship with Jesus, to which we are called. Are you saying—'If I were 21 today, Jesus would not be calling me to the priesthood'? I really don't think we can speak for Jesus like that! Or are you saying— 'If I were 21 today, I wouldn't say "Yes" to Jesus calling me to the priesthood (ie I would only relate with Jesus on my terms)'? It is very risky, even hypothetically, to think like that. It gives the Bad Spirit a way into the present moment, where he can appear as an angel of light.

This is how I replied:

> The matter of the call presumably is always to be seen in the context from which we can incarnate the presence of Jesus and discern the call of the Spirit. Presumably, we are *ad idem* in stating: If I were born into a Muslim family, I don't think I would be a priest today. If I were born a girl, I don't think I would be called to priesthood. Where we seem to part is in considering: If I were born into a social context where there were not the supports and encouragements to consider priesthood, and where the likely consequences of priesthood would be membership of an ageing and diminishing group serving a Church that was seen to be more dysfunctional and with a hierarchy more removed from the realities of ordinary people's lives, I don't think I would be so likely to discern a call to priesthood now as I would have in 1975.
>
> If your approach is right then of course, there are just as many young men now being called by the Spirit but they are ignoring the call. You would judge them as dealing with Jesus on their terms. If my approach is right, the Spirit is not calling as many young men to priesthood precisely because it is a very different call from what it was forty or sixty years ago. But you don't think we can speak for Jesus like that! I appreciate your caution about playing around with Jesus and making room for the Bad Spirit. But I am wary about any approach which passes adverse judgment on all those who have not answered 'the unchanging call' in the same numbers as they did in the

past. Existentially, it is now a very different call, in my view. And it is no surprise that so few are taking it up in our part of the world.

Either we have to judge adversely those who have not joined in the same numbers in the past or we have to re-assess the work of the Spirit in calling a reduced number to our ranks.

Given the shortage of priests and religious in the contemporary Australian church as compared with the situation fifty years ago, we need to provide more resources and opportunities to the laity wanting to perform the mission in Christ's name—lay organisations, public juridic persons, volunteering, better structured opportunities for part time commitment to the apostolate, and provision by religious orders for young people wanting to make a commitment for a few years before marriage and life and work in civic service.

The greatest challenge is providing a place in the Church for women wanting to contribute to the mission. It is high time to put institutional flesh on the bones of Pope Francis's unassailable claim stated in the sentence which was unwittingly omitted from the *America* version of the *La Civilta Cattolica* interview: 'It is necessary to broaden the opportunities for a stronger presence of women in the Church.'[23] He then went on to say:

> The woman is essential for the church. Mary, a woman, is more important than the bishops. I say this because we must not confuse the function with the dignity. We must therefore investigate further the role of women in the church. We have to work harder to develop a profound theology of the woman. Only by making this step will it be possible to better reflect on their function within the church. The feminine genius is needed wherever we make important decisions. The challenge today is this: to think about the specific place of women also in those places where the authority of the church is exercised for various areas of the church.[24]

---

23. See Dennis Coday, 'America' apologises for omission in Francis interview, *National Catholic Reporter*, 25 September 2013, at http://ncronline.org/news/vatican/america-apologizes-omission-francis-interview
24. *America*, 30 September 2013, 28

There's no getting away from the claim that anything less than full participation at all levels of leadership and service requires coherent scriptural and theological warrant. Authoritative declarations prohibiting discussion from hereon will only undermine the authority of the speaker and of the enforcers. Let's recall that the seventeen member Pontifical Biblical Commission concluded unanimously thir in 1976: 'It does not seem that the New Testament by itself alone will permit us to settle in a clear way and once and for all the problem of the possible accession of women to the presbyterate.' The minority of five members of that Commission thought that 'in the scriptures there are sufficient indications to exclude this possibility, considering that the sacraments of eucharist and reconciliation have a special link with the person of Christ and therefore with the male hierarchy, as borne out by the New Testament'. The majority of twelve members of that Commission wondered 'if the church hierarchy, entrusted with the sacramental economy, would be able to entrust the ministries of eucharist and reconciliation to women in light of circumstances, without going against Christ's original intentions'.[25] Admittedly, biblical interpretation is not a numbers game. But come on Francis, it's time for change. I know you have said the door is closed. But the door rather than the wall was a good image for you to choose. A door can be opened. It might still need a little prising and a lot of prayer.

Good news: The era of laity and willing liturgical celebration of life's sacramental moments

Wondering about this time in the Church, I looked back at a reflection I wrote eight years previously at the request of the legendary emeritus Professor Greg Dening who had been a Jesuit but later became an anthropologist and sociologist of culture. In 2006 he published a refreshing ethnographic history of the Jesuit parishes on the North

---

25. 'Can Women Be Priests?', Report From Pontifical Biblical Commission, *Origins*, Volume 6, Issue 6, 1 July 1976. The sidenotes of *Origins* state: 'Seventeen members present at the recent plenary session of the Pontifical Biblical Commission, voted on various aspects of the report appearing here. They agreed unanimously that the New Testament by itself does not seem able to settle in a clear way and once and for all whether women can be ordained priests. The members voted 12-5 that scriptural grounds alone are not enough to exclude the possibility of ordaining women.'

Shore of Sydney Harbour entitled *Church Alive*. He asked me to write a one-page reflection on priesthood. On re-reading it I decided I would need to change only the dates. This is what I wrote.

> I have been a Jesuit for thirty years (now forty years). I was ordained twenty years ago (now thiry years ago). Just before my ordination, a four-year-old niece reminded me that it was her birthday. The conversation went something like this: 'You won't give me a present, will you?' 'No'. (Given that I have twenty nieces and nephews, I thought this this the best policy for a Jesuit with a vow of poverty.) 'And that's because you're a priest, isn't it?' 'Yes'. 'When you're a man again, will you give me a present?'
>
> There is a real mystery to priesthood. That mystery can speak of grace but it doesn't always. Sometimes it is just strange and different.
>
> In the most routine parish daily Mass, there is a deep silence as you utter the words, 'This is a cup of my blood . . . It will be shed for you and for all so that sins may be forgiven.' (That was, you might remember what we used to say.) From the sanctuary, you behold a scattered faithful who are at that moment full of faith. And you know some of the stories behind the reverential postures before you. The abiding faith of these people sustains you in your own struggle for faith in a God who is with us and who cares enough to respond to our prayers, in blood.
>
> Then we pray for peace. The silence before the prayer formula is wide enough to hold all the battles of our world and the struggles, which each worshipper brings to the altar that day. As priest you see this, day in and day out, often having privileged access to those struggles.
>
> Then come the special moments of baptisms, weddings and funerals when the churched ones are like leaven in the loaf, carrying the structure of the liturgy, while the unchurched, through their awkwardness and unfamiliarity with the forms and words, look to you to carry it through. And you look back to them to know what and whom we celebrate on this occasion. It is special to be the vested embodiment of the connection between the citizens of an unchurched world that wonders if there is anything more than ritual to mark the passage of life, love and death, and the parishioners of a church which dares to offer the sacrament of Jesus to all comers, in season and out of season.

Here we can think of Manzoni's character—'the Unnamed". The globalisation of indifference makes us all 'unnamed', responsible, yet nameless and faceless.

Then on his visit to the Jesuit Church in Rome he said:

> After Lampedusa and other places of arrival, our city, Rome, is the second stage for many people. Often—as we heard—it's a difficult, exhausting journey; what you face can even be violent—I'm thinking above all of the women, of mothers, who endure this to ensure a future for their children and the hope of a different life for themselves and their family. Rome should be the city that allows refugees to rediscover their humanity, to start smiling again. Instead, too often, here, as in other places, so many people who carry residence permits with the words 'international protection' on them are constrained to live in difficult, sometimes degrading, situations, without the possibility of building a life in dignity, of thinking of a new future![28]

Some of this sounds like politics! In one of his regular, rambling weekday homilies in September, 2013 Francis made it clear that the gospel and politics do mix. Reflecting on the centurion who asked healing for his servant, Francis said that those who govern 'have to love their people,' because 'a leader who doesn't love, cannot govern—at best they can discipline, they can give a little bit of order, but they can't govern.' He mentioned 'the two virtues of a leader': love for the people and humility. 'You can't govern without loving the people and without humility! And every man, every woman who has to take up the service of government, must ask themselves two questions: 'Do I love my people in order to serve them better? Am I humble and do I listen to everybody, to diverse opinions in order to choose the best path.' If you don't ask those questions, your governance will not be good. The man or woman who governs—who loves his people is a humble man or woman.' Francis insisted that none of us can be indifferent to politics: 'None of us can say, 'I have nothing to do with

---

http://www.vatican.va/holy_father/francesco/homilies/2013/documents/papa-francesco_20130708_omelia-lampedusa_en.html

28. Pope Francis, *Address during the visit to the Astalli Centre*, the Jesuit Refugee Service in Rome (10 September 2013).

this, they govern. . . .' No, no, I am responsible for their governance, and I have to do the best so that they govern well, and I have to do my best by participating in politics according to my ability. Politics, according to the Social Doctrine of the Church, is one of the highest forms of charity, because it serves the common good. I cannot wash my hands, eh? We all have to give something!' He then became a little playful in his homily: 'A good Catholic doesn't meddle in politics.' That's not true. That is not a good path. A good Catholic meddles in politics, offering the best of himself, so that those who govern can govern. But what is the best that we can offer to those who govern?' He concluded: 'So, we give the best of ourselves, our ideas, suggestions, the best, but above all the best is prayer. Let us pray for our leaders, that they might govern well, that they might advance our homeland, might lead our nation and even our world forward, for the sake of peace and of the common good.'[29]

Our Catholic voice must be heard in season and out of season when it comes to laws and policies impacting on the poor, the vulnerable, and the marginalised—the poor, the widow and the orphan. We must not be afraid to mix it in the world. It's not as if our Catholic tradition gives us fixed answers to all problems but it equips us with principles and a culture well suited to seeking the good, the true and the beautiful in any situation. We are called in the Ignatian tradition to find God in all things, and to discern God's presence in the life of every person. In the interview for *La Civilta Cattolica* Francis said:

> If the Christian is a restorationist, a legalist, if he wants everything clear and safe, then he will find nothing. Tradition and memory of the past must help us to have the courage to open up new areas to God. Those who today always look for disciplinarian solutions, those who long for an exaggerated doctrinal 'security', those who stubbornly try to recover a past that no longer exists—they have a static and inward-directed view of things. In this way, faith becomes an ideology among other ideologies. I have a dogmatic certainty: God is in every person's life. God is in everyone's life. Even if the life of a person has been a disaster, even if it is destroyed by

---

29. Pope Francis, *Homily*, 16 September 2013, quoted in *Vatican Insider*, 16 September 2013 at http://vaticaninsider.lastampa.it/en/the-vatican/detail/articolo/27882/

vices, drugs or anything else—God is in this person's life. You can, you must try to seek God in every human life. Although the life of a person is a land full of thorns and weeds, there is always a space in which the good seed can grow. You have to trust God.[30]

And to cap it all off: on 17 September 2013, Francis was 'in attendance' in a simple white cassock, not presiding and not concelebrating, at the episcopal ordination Mass of the new papal almoner (the official distributor of alms), Archbishop Konrad Krajewski. Francis briefly put a stole around his neck and laid hands on the newly consecrated bishop.[31] You could almost hear the episcopal gasps and see the shock of the liturgists and canon lawyers from here on the other side of the globe! Fasten your seat belts. We are in for an exciting ride with this Pope. He's happy to make mistakes. He's happy to go with the flow. But above all, he is so happy in his own skin and in his religious tradition that he exudes the confidence that comes only from knowing that he is loved and forgiven, and not from thinking that he is always right and has all the answers.

Our credibility as Church has been enhanced with this new pope. We see in him many of the finest aspects of our presently battered and ageing Church. In the end we will only be as credible in the public square as we are credible with each other—pilgrims on the way who take radically seriously Jesus and his call, together with our varied life experiences and authentic reflections on those experiences. We will only be credible as an institution if we and especially our leaders are seen to be attentive and respectful to the competencies and insights of others. Our Church is presently a strained, outdated social institution with a hierarchy and clergy even more male dominated than an Abbott Cabinet. But it is also the privileged locus for us to be called to

---

30. *America*, 30 September 2013, 32.
31. *L'Osservatore Romano*, 19 September 2013. At the conclusion of the ceremony, 'the new bishop briefly greeted those present. "Today I would like to thank Pope Francis for his prayers and for his trust", he said, stressing that the Holy Father offers them "the opportunity to worship and touch Jesus in the poor, the abandoned, and the marginalised people. This allows me to discover the face of Jesus in my neighbour. He wants me to go in search of them without waiting for them to knock at the Vatican's door". "Your Holiness", he said, turning to the Pope, "I know that I have to be a priest of a basin and towel".

the banquet of the Lord sharing theology and sacrament which have sustained the hearts and minds of similar pilgrims for two millennia.

Speaking with *La Republica's* Eugenio Scalfari in October 2013, Francis shrugged off our minority status and present travails with this splendid summary of our mission which is the road back to credibility: 'We must be a leaven of life and love, and leaven is of an infinitely smaller quantity than the mass of fruit, flowers and trees that are born from that leaven. I think I said before that our objective is not to proselytise but to listen to needs, aspirations, disappointments, desperation and hopes. We must restore hope to the young, help the elderly, open up to the future and spread love. To be poor among the poor. We must include the excluded and preach peace. Vatican II, inspired by John XXIII and Paul VI, decided to look to the future with a modern spirit and to open up to modern culture. The Council Fathers knew that opening up to modern culture would mean religious ecumenism and dialogue with non-believers. Subsequently, however, little was done in that regard. I have the humility and ambition to want to do it.'[32] Let's join him.

Having thrown off the shackles of compulsion endured by pre-Vatican II Catholics, we relish that we come to the table not because we are forced, not because of social expectations, not because of the mindset of the mob, but because we are graciously called and freely responding. A while ago I was at a cocktail party and a very sophisticated woman said to me, 'I am not at all religious. And for me that's very good because I am free to think for myself and to make my own decisions.' I demurred: 'I am religious and from a Church that takes tradition and authority seriously. That does not mean that I do not think for myself nor that I do not make my own decisions. But I derive enormous benefit from being part of a community of thinkers and decision makers through the ages who wrestle with the hard questions. I find their experience and reflection on their experience helpful while I do my thinking and make my decisions.' Recently, I received a text message from one of my nieces about her six year old son Liam. It read: 'Late night tonight with fireworks. Driving home now and tired Liam says, "Mum if we sleep in, it's OK because we can

---

32. Reprinted in *L'Osservatore Romano*, 9 October 2013 and available on the Vatican website at http://www.vatican.va/holy_father/francesco/speeches/2013/october/documents/papa-francesco_20131002_intervista-scalfari_en.html

miss mass. I noticed you don't need to book into it.'" How right he is. We don't need to book, but all are welcome. It's good news for all, or at least that's what we believers tell ourselves in good faith. We're still gathering at the table of the banquet. We're still thinking and we're still making decisions that matter, ultimately. We have something to say and plenty to celebrate. We have duties to perform for the good of the Church and of the world, not because we are commanded by authority but because we are freely responding to the call of the One who came to give life to all, life to the full.

Contributors

Frank Brennan SJ, is an Australian Jesuit, professor of law at Australian Catholic University and Adjunct Professor at the Australian Centre for Christianity and Culture, the Australian National University College of Law and the National Centre for Indigenous Studies. His latest books are *No Small Change: The Road to Recognition for Indigenous Australia* and *Amplifying That Still, Small Voice*.

Chris Geraghty, is a retired judge of the District Court of New South Wales. He is the author of three memoirs of his time in the seminary and in the priesthood: *Cassocks in the Wildness—Remembering the Seminary at Springwood* (2001), *The Priest Factory—A Manly Vision of Triumph, 1958-1962 and Beyond* (2003), and *Dancing with the Devil—A Journey from the Pulpit to the Bench* (2012).

Michael Kelly SJ, Executive Director, UCAN, Thailand, is an Australian Jesuit who has worked in media since the 1970s in print, radio, TV and more recently in the Internet.

ATF Press Style Guide

1. *Indented material*: Indented quotations, of over 5 lines of material, or 30 words, should be indented on both sides. There should be a space of one line before and after the quotation. Quotations should not have quotation marks at the beginning or end and within the quotation there should be single quotation marks (exception: where *within* the indented quote there is a quote that is also quoting (. . . ' . . . " . . . " . . ' . . .).

2. *Headings*: Headings should not be numbered unless there is a particular need (for example, cross-referencing within the text, scientific or text-book style presentation. Capitals should be used for the initial letters only of headings and subsections (unless using proper nouns). Headings and subsections do not have punctuation at the end.

3. *Spelling*: The general guide to spelling will be taken from *The Macquarie Dictionary*. We use '-ise' forms for words (and not '-ize') (so: realise, globalisation, modernise . . .). Hyphens should be used in words such as 'co-operate' and 'co-ordinate', except where the mathematical 'coordinate' is used. *The Australian Writers Dictionary* is a valuable tool for assisting with the use of hyphens. We prefer World War 1 (and not First World War). All Latin, Greek and all foreign words should be in italics and have an English translation. We prefer transliterations of biblical languages but if biblical languages are used then the English must be given in brackets.

4. *Abbreviations and contractions*
Abbreviations are generally not used: editor (rather than ed.), translated by (rather than trans.), volume (rather than vol.), number (rather than no.), for example (not e.g.). Those such as USA or UN do not have full points between the letters. Contractions, which end in the last of the whole word, should not be given a full point: Dr (Doctor), St (Saint).

5. *Personal initials* Do not insert a stop or space between personal initials, as for example: AN Simple.

6. *Dates and numbers* Avoid unnecessary punctuation: 24 June 1999 (and not 24 June, 1999, or June 24th , 1999). 1990s (not 1990's). Twentieth century (not 20th century). When referring to the age of a person, 'she was in her eighties', use the spelt-out form, but use figures in the hyphenated form when writing of an '80-year-old woman'. In text use of year span: 1991–8 with an en rule (not hyphen and no space) (not 1991-8), 1902–3 (and not1902-03), 1878–83. When in headings or subsections, use 1990–1992. Financial years are 1991/92. Spans of numbers: use as few digits as possible, with the exception of 11–19, where 1 is repeated. So: 112–13,103–8, 34–9, 145–53. Numbers up to ninety-nine are spelt out in the text, except where figures are needed in a string of hyphenated words (35-hour week) or where figures will assist with clarity (when several numbers are compared). Numbers over ninety-nine are usually written in numerals but can be spelt out (about a thousand people) where figures seem inappropriate in the text. When a date is the first word of the sentence, use the spelt out form. Use figures for sums of money, $1.24, but three cents. Times should be in words rather than numerals when precision is not intended. So: 'They had to leave at three o'clock'. But where a precise time is intended: 'The bus leaves at 10.23am'. Percentages should be spelt out in the text: ninety-three per cent (note 'per cent'). But 93% in footnotes and tables.

7. *Hyphens and dashes*: En rules (a short dash) should be used for spans of numbers: 182–3; for Christian biblical references for the verses: Mk 3:12–13; for expressions of time: May–June; expressions of distance: Adelaide–Melbourne; and where 'and' is meant. Em rules (a long dash) are used in parenthetical statements, with no gap either side. For example, 'To have wide lawns—and not any garden—is not necessary for a happy life'.

8. *Quotations*: Indented quotes do not have opening and closing quotation marks. Short extracts of less than 5 lines (or 30 words) may appear within the text, enclosed in single quotation marks. Quotation marks should go inside the final full point if there is any authorial comment within the sentence; that is, the full point belongs to the author as part of her/his sentence. Time and time again, 'people do not speak' was quoted by authors. Or Sally was known to have said that 'the weather at the Cape is fine all year round'. If the quotation begins within a sentence containing authorial comment but runs to more than one sentence, it is acceptable to place the closing quotation mark after the final full point. George Stephens wrote with glee 'about fifty men broke out of the prison yesterday evening. We expect to have them rounded up before the week is past.' When a sentence is entirely quoted material, then all punctuation belongs to the quotation; therefore, the final full point goes inside the closing quotation mark. Mary received the telegram at 10 am. 'I never knew a darker moment than when I read of John's death.' Double quotation marks are only used for quotes within quotes. Eggs were thrown at the 'vote "No" for a republic' banner.

Indicate any omission from a quotation by the use of an ellipsis (. . .), with a single space keyed in before and after each point. Do not insert an additional full point if the ellipsis occurs at the end of a sentence. Do not use editorial caps within square brackets as in '[I]t is then . . . ', but leave the lower close letter, or adjust the way the quote is used.

9. *Footnotes*

Notes should be used for sources you have used, published or unpublished, to a brief discussion of the sources, to develop a point out of the text, or to cross reference to other parts of the text. Footnotes in the text should be used as a superscript text and in Times.

9.1 *Books*: First name (not initials) and surname, title of the book (in italics), place of publication, publisher and year (all in brackets), followed by page numbers. We do not use p or pp for footnote entries or in the text. In the text write word 'page' if necessary. In footnotes there is minimal punctuation: First reference:

Victor Pfitzner, *The Islands of Peru* (Adelaide: ATF Press, 1999), 21.

Second and subsequent references copy and paste name (surname only) and title of book (or abbreviated title), followed by page number. Where a title is long a suitable shorter version should be used in second and subsequent references.

Pfitzner, *The Islands of Peru*, 28.

9.2 *Articles in journals:* First name, surname, title of article, (with single inverted commas), title of the journal (in italics), volume and number, year (year in brackets), followed by a colon and then the pages of the article. We do not uses p or pp in footnotes or in the text. First reference: Victor Pfitzner, 'Where To From Here?', in *Interface: A Pyschology Review*, 1/2 (1998): 22–3.

Second and subsequent references: Pfitzner, 'Where to From Here?', 38.

9.3 *Articles in books:* First name, surname, title of article (with single inverted commas), edited by, with first name first, title of the book (in italics), place of publication, publisher and year (all in brackets), followed by a colon and then page. Victor Pfitzner, 'Yesterday, Today And Tomorrow', in *Readings in Contemporary History*, edited by Victor Pfitzner (Adelaide: ATF Press, 2002), 22–56. 9.4 *Web references*: First name, surname, title of article, web address enclosed in <…>, access date. Victor Pfitzner, 'Today and Not Tomorrow' at <www.newspoll.com.apost-au>. Accessed 20 July 2010. (No underlining).

10. *Bibliography*: We do not normally have a bibliography included with texts. But if one is to be used then, authors surname first, followed by initials and in alphabetical order of surname. Title of the book is in italics and with place of publisher, publisher and year in brackets. Pfitzner, V, *History of The New Time* (Adelaide: ATF Press, 2002).

Lightning Source UK Ltd.
Milton Keynes UK
UKOW01n0354080218
317519UK00003B/55/P